MENDING
THE EARTH

MENDING THE EARTH

A World for Our Grandchildren

edited by
Paul Rothkrug
and
Robert L. Olson

North Atlantic Books
Berkeley, California

The Environmental Rescue Fund
San Francisco, California

Mending The Earth: A World for Our Grandchildren
© 1991 by Paul Rothkrug and Robert L. Olson
Copyrights of individual pieces to their respective authors
ISBN 1-55643-091-4

Published by
North Atlantic Books
2800 Woolsey Street
Berkeley, California 94705
and
The Environmental Rescue Fund
1998 Broadway
San Francisco, California 94109

This is issue #43 of the *Io* series

Cover photo: Earthrise over the lunar horizon (Apollo X) NASA Photo
Cover and book design by Paula Morrison
Typeset by Campaigne & Associates Typography
Printed in the United States of America

Mending The Earth: A World for Our Grandchildren is sponsored by the
Society for the Study of Native Arts and Sciences, a nonprofit educational
corporation whose goals are to develop an educational and crosscultural
perspective linking various scientific, social, and artistic fields; to nurture a
holistic view of arts, sciences, humanities, and healing; and to publish and
distribute literature on the relationship of mind, body, and nature.

Library of Congress Cataloging-in-Publication Data
Mending the earth : a world for our grandchildren / edited by Paul
    Rothkrug and Robert L. Olson.
    p.   cm.
        ISBN 1-55643-091-4 : $9.95
        1. Environmental protection. 2. Human ecology. I. Rothkrug,
    Paul, 1915-   . II. Olson, Robert L. (Robert Linus), 1942-   .
    TD170 . M46   1990
    363 . 7–dc20   90-23408
                                                                          CIP

Table of Contents

Acknowledgements

An anthology like this is a cooperative effort, made possible only through the help of contributors, the publisher, and a circle of supportive friends. We are especially grateful to Shirley Rothkrug, Marge Olson, Gretchen Valido, Nancy Jack Todd, and Lindy Hough, whose suggestions shaped the book's content and improved the writing.

MENDING OUR WAYS

by Kathy Glass

In the heat of the summer afternoon, dry needles rain from the redwood canopy. It's not cool even here, in the depth of the forest. Many say the Earth's climate is changing: soon it may be undeniable. And every plant, every animal will feel the heat. As I look around the forest at the logged stumps of once-massive old-growth trees, I think: My time on the Earth is marked by this truth—I am living in the decline of the natural world as we know it. Forests, oceans, the atmosphere and other living species, nothing is exempt from the environmental deterioration, not even *Homo sapiens*, the "wise" species. It is as the Native Americans described: "Man did not weave the web of life, he is merely a strand in it. Whatever he does to the web, he does to himself."

My time is marked by another fact: In the next few decades, my culture will have reached a consensus on reversing the deterioration of its habitat, or it will be irrevocably committed to extinction. It seems like a simple decision, and yet many say the necessary changes are too hard, too costly to make. Or that "the American people aren't ready for them."

Here in the land of the free, we are dulled by middle-class comforts, by TV and alcohol and job stress and advertising pressure to consume, to be one of the beautiful people. So much competes for our fragmented attention, it's hard to see beyond the confines of our own desires. In many ways the task before us is not so much saving the Earth as it is delivering ourselves from hype. Amid such materialism and unsatiated desire, how are we to grasp the global implications of our collective acts, much less intuit the sacred in our natural world? Where is the connection to be made?

Such connections, of course, are up to each individual. Our environmental problems are rooted in a spiritual crisis, a lack of perception, an inappropriate relationship with the land and the beings that share it with us. To reverse the trend of environmental destruction, we must alter our selves profoundly. That's why my time on Earth is also full of promise and excitement: Nothing less than a total revolution in consciousness and lifestyle can save us.

Already there are strong harbingers of change among the people. The emerging ecocrisis catalyzes a powerful desire for a positive vision of the future. This crisis makes national boundaries and political disputes of secondary importance, because we are all in the same boat on this one. Excellent, practical ideas and new technologies abound; many are discussed in this book. Many alternatives are already available. The problem is overcoming individual apathy and governmental and corporate paralysis. What will it take?

One need not be a scientist or psychic to see that our problems are already immense. We need more than eco-freak friends urging us to recycle, to avoid styrofoam products, to take public transit instead of the car once in a while. Individual actions are important, of course—they are the basis of a sustainable way of life. But people need leadership. They need to do their part in a larger effort, not struggle against the prevailing current. Whether one acts as an individual or a business, making changes for environmental reasons becomes much easier if there is a supporting network. Providing a larger, more open framework for change and strong leadership in this effort is also what this book is about.

We don't need more facts or exhortations. We need immediate action. We need sacrifices of personal convenience and corporate profit, in the knowledge that such changes are not sacrifices as much as they are long-term investments—and that truly we have no choice. The bill is overdue. The level of resource consumption maintained in this country cannot possibly be extended to all nations, and yet our standard of living is what so many others aspire to. This is simple to see. We need to take the initiative for change and set a global example.

For all its innovation and accomplishments, our culture has a severely limited vision. Growth and profit at any cost is not even good business—many industries (such as the timber industry) cut their own throats by operating rapaciously and unsustainably. Some businesses market weapons and bombs internationally only to stare down the barrels of their own product. Others manufacture deadly chemicals that will eventually lace the food consumed by its own employees. These have to be signs of a stagnant civilization.

The corporate and governmental response to the environmental crisis has until now been totally inadequate. Why aren't the stakes acknowledged? Business as usual continues as pollution controls and conservation measures are fought on every front. Protecting the profit margin is one issue, but certainly businesspeople and the politicians they buy have children, too. They breathe the same air and drink the same water. Their mothers and brothers die of cancer, the land around them is increasingly paved with asphalt and concrete, their food is contaminated, the trees fall and waterways are thick with slime. Not to feel this poisoning of life is simply not to feel. Can anyone think he or she is exempt?

There are things in life more real than money and leisure; there are more creative endeavors than simply turning a profit. The time has come for each individual to ask if he or she is a slave to greed and desire, or if he can aspire to something better. That is the real bottom line. I am thinking especially of our leaders, of the powerful and wealthy, because if they can't value life and land more than money, our civilization is indeed lost and no amount of grassroots organizing can save us.

Material possessions and ease of existence are not the goals of human life on Earth. If you need to ask what the real point is, you are probably part of the problem. If you can't remember the last time you sat by a flowing river or silently watched waves break on a beach or looked up with awe at the canopy of an ancient forest, you're probably out of touch.

Life is a quest for wholeness, and that involves identification with one's natural environment. If you realize your part in the whole, you don't do violence to it. Such admonitions may sound abstract or peripheral. But unless your actions, your business, your politics work for the Earth, not against it, you are in conflict with life itself, with your self, and with your children's future.

Mending the Earth is within our grasp, it is critical, it is a challenge, and there is probably a profit to be turned in the task as well, as chapters in this book illustrate. We are a creative society with tremendous intellectual assets. Will a botched job of existence be our legacy? Mending our ways and healing the ecosystem is not simply a trend or a business option—it is a survival strategy. You can buy in or bow out, but your decision affects every strand in the web we call life.

Foreword

MENDING THE EARTH,
MENDING OURSELVES

by Nancy Jack Todd

In her book, *The March of Folly*, the historian Barbara Tuchman ascribes the following criteria to her definition of folly: "the pursuit of given policies or actions perceived as counterproductive in their own time, not merely by hindsight," that such policies "belong to a group and not just an individual," and that they "persist beyond any political lifetime." In short, according to Barbara Tuchman, "folly is perverse persistence in a policy demonstrably unworkable or counterproductive." She was moved to write the book, she explained, because of "the ubiquity of the problem in our time." Expanding on her theme, she enumerates a series of the well known blunders of the past, the Trojan horse for example, questioning what form of misjudgment possessed the leaders of Troy to "drag a suspicious looking wooden horse inside their walls despite every reason to suspect a Greek trick." Concluding her list of many of the prominent and disastrous mistakes in judgment throughout history she poses the question: "why does American business insist on growth when it is demonstrably using up the three basics of life on our planet—land, water, and unpolluted air?"

Is the pursuit of folly innate to our species? The creatures of the natural world, with a few obvious exceptions like the lemmings exhibit, on the whole, a sturdier sense of survival. Or is there a possibility that we may come to our senses and not only begin to understand the cause and extent of our folly but take realistic, radical, and sufficient measures to leave a livable environment as our legacy to those who will follow us? The extensive and enthusiastic observation of Earth Day 1990 was heartening and hopeful. Concern for the environment now seems vastly greater than it has been. Beyond the reaches of the media, snatches of conversation on the subject can be heard almost everywhere, in supermarkets and post offices, restaurants and shops, even in as unlikely places as beauty parlors and exercise classes. There are already those optimistic enough to venture the opinion that the tide might be about to turn in terms of human abuse of the natural world and that, environmentally speaking, things might gradually begin to get better. Others are more pessimistic. They are worried that we might have reached or passed critical thresholds in such areas as atmospheric pollution or soil depletion and erosion, and that certain trends, global warming for one, might have become irreversible. The current rash of environmental enthusiasm might, they feel, be too little or too late.

On the other hand, prophesy these days, gloomy or otherwise, is a risky business. Who possibly could have called the odds on the sequence of events with which the eighties ended and the nineties began? Who would have dared to predict, in a period of months, the fall of dictatorship and the end of rule by force in Eastern Europe, the crumbling of the Berlin Wall, the end of single party rule in Russia, and the rebirth of hope throughout much of Europe? The overall pattern of present events—tumultuous for once does not seem an overblown adjective—has yet to reveal itself sufficiently clearly for pronouncements of either salvation or doom or something falling somewhere between the two.

The full story has yet to unfold. That many people are starting not only to care about the environment but to take effective action is a comparatively recent phenomenon. The microbiologist Lynn Margulis corroborated this recently observing: "We know how to detoxify polluted lakes, to compost garbage to form organically rich soil, and to reduce toxins. What is more, many people have started to do these things."

This statement is further substantiated by the fact that increasingly people are also replanting and restoring forests, detoxifying rivers and streams, planting deforested and eroded areas, setting aside large tracts of land for conservation and preserving wetlands and marshes. In addition to this kind of healthy public activism, as non-polluting and non-toxic products become increasingly available, it is becoming easier on a personal and household level to curb one's environmental impact. Lester Brown of the Worldwatch Institute has warned : "No attempt to protect the environment will be successful in the long run unless ordinary people—the California housewife, the Mexican peasant, the Soviet factory worker, the Chinese farmer are willing to adjust their lifestyles. Our wasteful, careless ways must become a thing of the past, We must recycle more, procreate less, turn off lights, use mass transit, do a thousand things differently in our everyday lives."

It is becoming better understood that, although our environmental problems are supranational and global in scope as are many of the solutions, the environmental crisis is also an internal and personal crisis. It is a crisis of conscience and of spirit within the individual, the household, and the community. And it is the totality of these that constitutes impending ecological disaster. It follows that it is with the individual, the household and the community that truly fundamental change begins. The less than glamorous commitment of such everyday ecological activities as facing one's organic garbage may be less than appealing. But spreading rich black compost on a garden is as satisfying as the avoidance of dangerous chemical fertilizers. Recycling, driving less, altering one's habits of consumption and energy use may not be wildly fulfilling in themselves, but as part of an ongoing, conscious practice of environmental awareness and stewardship, they can be attended by a quietly satisfying sense of participation. The feeling is limited only by the scope of the vision inspiring it. For those who have chosen to become involved in such personal or household commitments, or to devote themselves to the protection or restoration of a river or shoreline, a woods or meadow or some threatened species of plant or wildlife, a sense of partnership with the natural world tends to become a part of the experience of life.

There is strong evidence currently on the side of a more comprehensive appreciation of environmental problems among leaders of government and industry as well as the public. But beyond the most pressing efforts at cleanup, restoration, and waste reduction there will come the more difficult and serious task of the long term reevaluation of how we, as one species among billions, are to continue to live on our home planet. It has become fashionable in discussing environmental issues to quote some variation on Einstein's pronouncement that, with the advent of atomic weapons, everything has changed except the way we think. A change in terms of how we think about the human place in the natural world is obviously both urgent and overdue. Microbiologist Lynn Margulis is succinct and unsentimental on the subject. She defines us—human beings—as "peculiar slaves of the biosphere." By this she means that the natural world, biological life on Earth, had been evolving for billions of years before our remotest ancestors constituted themselves in any form recognizable as human. As humbling as may be, it is further believed by many biologists that biological life on the planet will continue to function, if in a drastically altered state, should we as a species be either so stupid or so rash as to eliminate the biological base for human survival.

Seen from this perspective, a change in the way we think about ourselves in relation to the Earth becomes less academic exercise than survival strategy. At issue is not only the philosophical and ecological challenge of how to create sustainable societies, but how to learn to live fully and richly within environmentally dictated constraints, and within such constraints, to rediscover or reinvent the meaning of being human in the context of the world of nature.

Interestingly, and perhaps not entirely coincidentally, a scientific theory has recently and rapidly been gaining credence that has the potential to change the way we think about the natural world. The Gaia theory, which is named for the ancient Greek goddess of the Earth, originated with two internationally recognized scientists, atmospheric chemist, James Lovelock, of England and microbiologist Lynn Margulis of the University of Massachusetts. This revolutionary theory suggests that the Earth, together with its atmosphere, is a living entity that functions systemically as an integrated whole. According to James Lovelock, Gaia is "a complex entity, involving the biosphere, atmosphere, oceans and soil; the totality constituting a feedback of cybernetic systems which seeks an optimal physical and chemical environment for life on this planet." Gaia theory sees the Earth as maintaining homeostatic conditions over vast reaches of geological time as a result of the activity of microbial life and the biota which seek to maintain the environment as optimal for life. Dr Lovelock describes such activity or processes as follows: "the physical and chemical condition of the surface of the Earth, of the atmosphere, and of the oceans has been and is actively made fit and comfortable by the presence of life itself. This is in contrast to the conventional wisdom which held that life adapted to the planetary conditions as it and they evolved their separate ways."

Implicit in Gaia theory is a potential paradigm for modern, scientifically schooled cultures yet to see the human role in planetary history as an ennobling one. We have the option to see and to choose to live our lives in the service of the larger life of the planet, to reaffirm the world that is, in James Lovelock's words, "built on the breath and bones and blood of our ancestors." There is no need for a split between mind and heart or intellect and spirit in coming to understand our role as participatory in a process that is at once ancient and mysterious, yet scientifically valid and imbued with the potential of teaching us how to live. Rather than seeing ourselves as peculiar slaves, we have the option of seeking our identity as participatory Earth stewards in coevolution with the Earth itself, with what Poet Gary Snyder called that great biosphere-being—Gaia.

Such a conceptual framework is vital to the far-reaching changes that will have to be made to avoid environmental disaster. A conceptual framework is so much a part of the way we think, as fundamental as the air we breathe, that it is invisible to most of us. Changing the underlying precepts people have about themselves and the world around them can take generations. And now time is short and the situation desperately urgent. The fantasy worlds of adventure stories are less necessary these days. We are living our cliffhanger. If we are to continue it is essential, as we struggle to adjust to a changing world view, to begin to articulate the fundamental assumptions of cultures that will be sustainable in the future. We must find ways of working with and informing children, young people, and each other. Far-reaching, and radical, efforts in education of all kinds is a major priority.

A renewed sense of intimacy with the natural world is one answer, although of limited applicability given the restricted opportunities for so many people in urban ares. Environmentalist Rachel Carson believed that a love of the natural world is best begun in childhood and that "To keep alive the sense of wonder needs the companionship of at least one adult who can share it, rediscovering with them the joy, excitement and mystery of the world we live in." Another founder of the environmental movement, Rene Dubos, once claimed that our greatest disservice to our children was to give them the belief that ugliness was somehow normal. As environmental educator David Orr maintains "Ugliness signifies a fundamental disharmony between people and people and people and the land." Here perhaps are a few useful clues for those of us with children in our lives, even if we are not officially cast as teachers or educators. The boundless curiosity of children about everything around them is an open door for older people with a love or knowledge of wildlife, of birds or flowers, of woodland walks, or fishing, or excursions to the country or the sea. Any effort expended will enrich children so favored not only for the moment but for a lifetime. And when this is not possible children can often still be shown some fragment of beauty or natural life even in limited and crowded conditions and be encouraged to cherish it, and strive to preserve it.

Beyond personal ties, the educational system is not giving children any sense of what environmental educator David Orr terms "ecological literacy." He refers to the critique of holocaust survivor Elie Wiesel who decried the education that created Nazi Germany which had "emphasized theories instead of values, concepts rather than human beings, abstraction rather than consciousness, answers instead of questions, ideology and efficiency rather than consciousness." The ecology of an inch of topsoil, David Orr points out, is still largely unknown, as is its relationships to the larger systems of the biosphere. It is his belief that it is not more information that is needed now, nor more education, unless it is education of a certain kind.

The kind of education appropriate to our moment would emphasize a sense of place, by which is meant that children and young people should know the basic ecology natural history of the areas in which they live. Even in cities they should learn characteristic geographic features and ecosystems and what makes their region unique, whether it be coastal, mountain, prairie, or farming country. Urban children can draw on this to see their lives as part of the world around them, with every effort being made to make such learning as experiential as possible. One innovative city program in the Boston area has undertaken what they are calling a television and field laboratory approach to environmental education. Basic to their idea is to instill in children and students the conviction that a sustainable future is possible. Their television series will include, as role models, examples of children and adults who have succeeded in making a difference in many kinds of environmental projects. They will draw on scientists and other experts, teachers, students and cartoon characters to carry their message and encourage participation. They also plan extensive field trips and studies that will utilize a mobile laboratory to provide a link between field site and classroom. Interactive video disc stations and computer networks will be set up for students to exchange information and work collaboratively with young people in other areas. Such innovative use of technology is just one way to bring the wider world to urban children. The costs should be seen as an investment in the future not only for those involved but for all who eventually benefit from a greater collective understanding of environmental processes.

David Orr is comprehensive in his suggestions for curriculum revision at all levels. He suggests that the household, school, campus, and region be brought into focus and examined as part of an ecosystem. Everyone should know as a matter of course, where in each case, food, energy, water, and materials come from, and at what human and ecological cost? Where do waste and garbage go and at what cost? He advocates a detailed study of institutional resource flows coupled with one of alternatives that may be more humane, ecologically sustainable, cheaper, and possibly more directly beneficial for regional economies. Conservation and recycling should be investigated as well as the buying power of an institution to determine whether it could better be used to support local enterprises. The argument goes that this type of study of resource flows leads to an examination of basic issues of human survival, life being, as David Orr has pointed out, the only defensible foundation for education.

The ultimate goal of education for children—and for all of us—would be a deep sense of participation in and responsibility for the world, comparable to that traditionally held by indigenous peoples. A number of years ago a Brazilian film entitled "Black Orpheus" transposed this kind of belief system to the a modern urban context, and did so most poignantly. In the film, from his barrio outside Rio de Janiero, Orpheus went at dawn to the edge of the sea to play his guitar. It was important that he do this, he explained to the local children, to make sure that the sun would rise each day. The morning after his death, still numb at the loss of their hero, the children remembered what he had told them about the sun coming up each day. They went to Orpheus's hut and got his guitar then stumbled along the path to the cliff overlooking the sea. With Orpheus gone, they knew it fell to them to keep the world going.

Elie Weisel analyzed the degree of disaster he feels can result from an emphasis on abstraction rather than consciousness in education. The thinking underlying programs like those advocated by David Orr, in expanding our intimate grasp of process in natural systems, would lead to an entirely different perspective. Degrees of magnitude more illusive than attempting to direct the course of human events is the personal and immediate experience of the continuing mystery of the living Earth itself. Among the most dramatic witnesses to the compelling nature of such an awakened sense of wonder are the astronauts and cosmonauts whose ventures into space seemed to have transformed their perceptions of the Earth and their sense of self in relation to it. One astronaut, Sigmund Juhn of East Germany has been quoted as "seeing the Earth in all its ineffable beauty and fragility." Equally evocative was the experience of reentry and landing described by Andryan Nikolayev of Russia who found the wind "delightful" after long days in space and the smells of Earth "unspeakably sweet and intoxicating." He recalls being filled then with "a strange feeling of complete, almost solemn contentment."

For the astronauts, it took leaving the Earth and seeing it hanging luminous and alive in the vastness of space to affect them profoundly. For the rest of us it may be a growing awareness of the possibility of losing the chance to be a continuing part of the unfolding story of Earth to jolt our consciousness and hone our behavior to practices more appropriate to our continuing coevolution as part of a living planet. This is a far from sentimental or simplistic prescription. In long range pragmatic terms, it has survival value. In an esthetic and spiritual context, Gaian thinker James Lovelock claims: "Any living organism a quarter as old as the universe itself and still full of vigor is as near immortal as we ever need to know. She is of this universe and, conceivably, a part of God. On Earth she is the source of life everlasting and is alive now: she gave birth to humankind and we are part of her."

At the end of the book *Myths and Texts* in referring to "that great biosphere being, Gaia," poet Gary Snyder asks: "What does the Earth, Gaia, in this great space, think she's doing? But what she does is not really our concern. Our concern is the shimmering network of gift exchange, the ceremonies of life; energy, transformation. Our concern is the kids sleeping in the back room, snow on the far hills, a coyote howling in the sagebrush moonlight."

I have found it useful, every few years or so, to go back to this passage of Gary Snyder's and rework it with reference to our own lives at a given time. At this juncture of planetary environmental awakening it seems appropriate for us to think of our day to day concern as: the ongoing struggle to have an impact as benign as possible on the larger world, to make ever more diverse and fertile and beautiful the valley in which we live, to bring renewed dedication to our projects of ecological restoration and to communicate the inherent sustainability of ecological design, to follow a course of hope rather than despair, and to remember the lives of children yet to come in all that we do.

And yours?

INTRODUCTION

> To feel much for others and little for ourselves . . . to restrain our selfish, and indulge our benevolent affections, constitutes the perfection of human nature.
>
> Adam Smith
> *The Theory of Moral Sentiments*

It is hard to face, but the truth is that we are ruining the world of our grandchildren. Their whole way of life is threatened by global environmental problems like ozone depletion and climate change. Widespread problems such as soil erosion, deforestation, water scarcity, and air pollution are already beginning to limit options for the future.

This book is written in the belief that there is still time to turn these problems around and create a world worthy of our grandchildren. But far-reaching social change, political action and technological innovation must be initiated here in the United States during the 1990s, before worsening problems create a sense of panic, precluding a rational political response.

The changes we need all have a common character that can be illustrated by a personal story.

Many years ago one of us bought a comfortable house on a quiet street in a neighborly New England town, a house where kids could grow up, where school chums could sleep over, where friends and neighbors could gather. It was our family home. We had shade trees, flowering shrubs, green grass, room for an outdoor gym and a game of touch football. In a time before air conditioning, the shade trees kept us cool in summer and eased the winter wind. They also kept the grass from growing in the front yard, so that rains left it a mess. Year after year we would resow with "shady lawn seed" and much fertilizer. The trees thrived; the shade grew thicker, and by

Decoration Day the grass was dead.

Finally, one spring, the handyman said, "Why not try some ground cover that needs shade?" And we did, and, lo, the trees and the pacasandra flourished together!

When all else failed, we finally broke out of the rigid mindset that "A proper house should have grass in the front yard" and tried the obvious: we grew something different!

It seems to us there is a lesson in this simple story that applies to our worsening environmental problems. Stuck in an inflexible mindset, we keep trying to grow on the pattern of the past. But the harder we try to grow, the worse environmental problems become. Some suggest giving up on growth, but in a world with rapidly expanding populations, terrible poverty, and environmentally unsound ways of doing things already in place, that would be a mess. The costs of growth are increasingly intolerable, but the costs of no-growth are unacceptable. So we need to break out of our inflexible mindset and try the obvious: we need to grow something different!

All the contributors to this book are interested in growing something different—environmentally-friendly advanced technologies, an energy-efficient economy, ecologically healthy cities, and new ecologically sound industries with new investments, new profits, and new markets worldwide.

They all want to build a new kind of *sustainable society* in which we can meet our own needs without endangering the prospects of future generations.

If we are to "grow something different," we need change on at least five fronts.

1. *A Focus on the Long-Term Common Interest*—There is no remedy for our problems within a mindset that constantly promotes short-term self-interest over the long-term common interest. We need a social emphasis on creating that better world for our grandchildren—all the grandchildren. We need to understand what Adam Smith understood: that a market economy produces a good society to the degree that people are able to restrain their selfishness and act out of benevolent affections.

2. *Environmentally Advanced Technologies*—In the environmental debates of the 1970s and 1980s, positions often polarized between technological optimists and critics of advanced technology. Again, there is no remedy for our problems within this kind of polarized mindset. We need technologies in every area of the economy that are simultaneously more productive and more in harmony with the environment. We need to develop the full potential of modern science and guide the evolution of technology with ecological values.

3. *Investment Opportunities*—There is no way to create a sustainable society without the full contribution of the private sector. The angry split that often exists between environmentalists and business leaders has to be mended. Everyone has to come out of their bunkers and learn to work together. We have to continue to offer legitimate investment and profit opportunities. Investment in restructuring the economy to preserve the environment will also give us greater security against "oil shocks" and increase our economic competitiveness.

4. *A More Informed and Active Electorate*—Overwhelming majorities want more done about environmental problems, and growing majorities say they are willing to pay for it. To galvanize change, we need a political struggle that revitalizes our political parties and brings millions of new voters into the electoral process. There will always be structures of wealth and power that benefit from things as they are, that do not want to give up their special privileges, and so resist change. But thanks to the wise design of our constitutional system, the power of "we the people" can counter the power of special interests.

5. *Attention to the Third World*—Many of the worst ecological problems in the world, like desertification and the loss of tropical forests, are caused by poverty. To solve these problems, and to allow the Third World to invest along with us in an environmentally sound future, we must help create a more

equitable international economic order. Under present rules of the game, wealth is continually flowing from the poor countries of the Third World to the rich industrial nations. Changing those global rules needs to become a top priority in our own national politics.

Sustainability, fairness, renewal, efficiency, visionary leadership and entrepreneurship, technical and social innovation, community, stewardship, grass roots political struggle, economics connected to social and ecological realities, a global perspective—these are the themes that appear again and again in the essays in this volume. They are themes for a new, mainstream post-Cold War politics in the 1990s.

We hope that you, our readers, will be helped to join the common struggle to mend the earth and, in so doing, bring forth a better society, a human community able to be guardians of the world of our grandchildren and worthy at last to be stewards of life on Earth.

Paul Rothkrug
Robert L. Olson.

Section I

Toward a Life-Sustaining Environment—Public Policy for Transition

Chapter 1

A PROGRAM FOR ACTION

by Paul Rothkrug

Stewardship

Contrary, cantankerous human behavior is creating this great historic dilemma: although change is the norm of nature, our never-ending search for security entails such resistance to change that we accept it only in the face of compelling necessity. Concurrently we are experiencing the law of physics called *inertia:* a body at rest tends to remain at rest; a body in motion tends to remain in motion. We acknowledge this principle regularly when we say "If you want something done, give it to a busy person," i.e., a body already in motion. To recognize and act on the interdependence of these two principles of nature would be to release the explosive potential behind increasing worldwide concern for the environment, applying the knowledge and technology now available to create a sustainable life for future generations on this Earth.

Sustainability is not something that can be quantified, despite the efforts of many leading economists to do so. A Dutch economist (H.J.M. de Vries) has put his finger on it: **"Sustainability is not something to be *defined*, but to be *declared*. It is an ethical guiding principle."** We hope to help start the process of change, understanding that once change begins inertia becomes our ally. We are the first civilization with sufficient knowledge to develop a comprehensive program for survival. We need to find the economic discipline and the political will to carry it out. The components of the struggle to resolve the crisis are many and will evolve over the next gen-

3

eration or two into a completely changed relationship between humanity and its planet. Alone of all forms of life, human beings have attempted to control the processes of nature; however, without an adequate understanding of the complex interplay of the myriad facets of the Earth's ecosystem. The scope of the needed change can be put very simply: we must move from exploitation to stewardship in all aspects of our relationship, not only to the planet, but to all forms of life which it supports, above all in our relationship to one another and all peoples of Earth.

As the nineties begin scientific consensus is telling us that, absent change, we shall reach an ecological point of no return in about 40 years which will involve collapsing economies, disappearing food supplies, social disintegration and other disasters.*

The invariable response from polluters to requests for change is that it would "cost too much." Cost is a pejorative word in our society. It brings up the specter of higher taxes, job changes and other uncomfortable adjustments in our way of life. Cost is but one side of the coin whose other side is value. We know this instinctively and act upon it when we approve of a "cost" which brings us something that we want. The diffuse, unfocused awareness of environmental priorities have not yet brought home to most of us, with sufficient clarity, the value to be received so as to generate an effective demand for change.

There was a time Americans were prepared to make sacrifices to bring about desirable change. There was a time when we could take the long view. Out of that long view came the settlement and development of an entire continent and the building of the most successful society in terms of meeting human needs that this planet has yet seen. There are those (good Americans) who would quarrel with that statement. They point to the disappearance of the native Americans, not to the point of extinction but as a part of our culture. They decry the turbulent conquest of a continent, the violence, the waste, the bloodshed.

---

* In order to present a coherent development of our thinking and suggestions, we have placed source material and detailed analysis in a separate section at the end of the general discussion. (Editors)

It has been said that if you would change a thing, you first must love it. If there is much that is ugly in our history, to be an American is nothing to be ashamed of. Ours is the story of the rebirth of freedom on this earth, after a lapse of over two thousand years since the disappearance of ancient Greek democracy.

Birth is never a pretty thing. It is pain and blood and screaming, but it is the miracle of creation all over again every time. So let it be with America. We brought freedom back to this world. We brought it with a thunderclap whose reverberations still echo over the span of centuries. *The message here is that we use that freedom to lead humanity, and all living things, on the path to survival.*

Perhaps not more than 10% of the over five billion people now inhabiting the earth are working for more than bare subsistence. It would take a doubling, at least, of the productive work force of the globe to bring about the development of the vast new industries needed to halt and reverse environmental decay. Adding 500 million or so productive workers would produce new value beyond anything dreamed of in the past, with the potential for bringing the whole world to higher living standards. The process would bring with it very substantial social and economic changes. **It would require a return to the long view.**

When we look at the pejorative word "cost" from that perspective, it becomes apparent that the opposition to change is not really based on cost but on one's "comfort level." We like things as they are.

A major part of things as they are entails vast waste. The profligate who wastes and dissipates his patrimony without thought of tomorrow is considered a fool and looked upon with contempt. Yet we live in a civilization which collectively is doing exactly that. In the 300 years since the beginning of the Industrial Revolution the so-called "advanced societies" have managed to dissipate resources accumulated on the planet in the past three billion years.

The accepted level of wasted energy for the U.S. economy is 75%. Every BTU* we use could be made to produce four times the amount of work it now does. In dollars that amounts to something

---

* British Thermal Unit.

5

between 250 and 300 billion per year, **after** allowing for the cost of more efficient techniques and installations.

In spite of threats like the Iraq crisis, in the new atmosphere of a post-Cold War world we can safely cut our defense budget in half. That gives us a total efficiency bonus of 400 to 450 billions **annually** to start the process of change. That figure is also the measure of profits unearned and unwarranted by any understanding of social value.

Now we know what the power structure really means when they tell us the transition will "cost" too much. They mean that profits from waste are easier to come by than the earnings from socially productive enterprise. To that 400 billion dollar annual waste bill we still have to add the cost of the non-renewable resources despoiled over three centuries to grasp the extent of what the so-called "free market" has exacted from society.

Another price that we pay for our waste of resources is a reduction in the competitiveness of our economy in relation to other developed nations. For example, Japan's use of energy per unit of gross national product is approximately 30% of ours.

There is much evidence that global warming has already begun: the '80s produced the highest average range of temperatures in weather bureau records. We are washing topsoil into the sea; we are losing irrigated land to salt and chemical build-up. Annual grain production has begun to fall *absolutely*, let alone failing to keep up with population growth. The world is losing 24 billion tons of topsoil each year for an annual compound loss of 6% of grain production, in the face of an annual population increase of 1.8%. The pollution of irrigated land worldwide costs humanity another 1.25% compounded annually in grain yield. The United States is not excluded. In 1989 domestic consumption of grain exceeded production for the first time in history, and we had to draw on reserve stocks. *We face the specter of mass starvation the world over.*

"Compelling necessity" is upon us, and even those who are reluctant to change will have to make way for the new relationship between humanity and its planet: the rising ground swell of public opinion will inevitably change the political landscape of America. It becomes the task of those leading the movement for change to keep the dysfunctional economic and social aspects of change within tolerable limits until the beneficial results of the change continuum itself begin to take effect.

Our Constitution provides the framework for orderly democratic procedures which can accomplish the transition to a sustainable future, with full consideration for the welfare of all. However, our political establishment has been consistently unresponsive to the consequences of ongoing environmental damage. It may be useful to refer to what Felix Rohatyn, a leading Wall Street investment banker and chairman of the Municipal Assistance Corporation for New York City, told the Women's National Democratic Club on March 15th:

> "The Republican Party is internationalist and expansionary militarily and economically; it is rigorously conservative, if not to say reactionary, on social issues such as abortion, school prayer, gun control, etc.; it is dedicated to the pursuit of wealth through lower taxes and absence of regulation without any seeming concern for the appropriate role of government. What does the Democratic Party stand for, as an alternative to this program? It is exceedingly hard to tell because the Democrats are not an opposition party. **The Democrats share power, they do not seek it.*** Seeking power requires submitting alternatives to the voters and competing for their allegiance; sharing power is an entirely different role. The Democratic leaders in the Congress are men of intellect and character, of decency and strength. But, they are part of an existing power structure, almost a coalition government with a Republican administration." (*Wall Street Journal*, March 15, 1990)

Lincoln's awesome question at Gettysburg: "Can a nation so dedicated and so consecrated long endure?" is once again on the agenda. Were the founding fathers naive in their estimate of human nature and in the ability or ordinary people to govern themselves? Is humanity now doomed to be governed by a "congress" of multinational corporations under a facade of so-called "democracy" whose office holders are dependent upon corporate funds for their entire careers?

---

* Emphasis added.

7

James Madison (hardly a wild-eyed visionary) at the Constitutional Convention in the summer of 1787 spoke of "this great republican principle, that the people will have virtue and intelligence to select men of virtue and wisdom."

Madison's use of the word virtue makes it a close synonym for what we would today call "common sense."

He continued, "Is there no virtue among us? If there be not, we are in a wretched situation. No theoretical checks, no form of government, can render us secure. To suppose any form of government will secure liberty or happiness without any virtue in the people, is a chimerical idea. If there be sufficient virtue and intelligence in the community, it will be exercised in the selection of these men; **so that we do not depend on their virtue, or put confidence in our rulers, but in the people who are to choose them....**

"Ambition must be made to counteract ambition. The interest of the man must be connected with the constitutional rights of the place. It may be a reflection on human nature that such devices should be necessary to control the abuses of government. But what is government itself but the greatest of all reflections on human nature?"

Far from being naive, the men of 1787 were only too conscious of the frailties of human nature. In the end they set up a government and a Constitution that relied on the free expression of a free and informed electorate for its operation and its very existence. They felt that the only true guarantee of freedom was an electorate where each voter voted his or her own convictions and the sum of all these free expressions would result in legitimate government. Now, however, with the power structure having taken control of the main channels of information, the foundation for a "free and informed" electorate must be re-established.

An informed electorate is one that is acquainted with the issues affecting the lives of its members. Different issues will draw different levels of response from different sections of the people. To raise the awareness of people and to motivate them to vote, we must analyze the issues and evaluate the levels of impact for different groups of the population. (Details in the next section and the appendix). Felix Rohatyn has defined "power structure" as government by the moneyed interests. There is an old fashioned name for that: "plutocracy."

A noted conservative commentator tells us, "The 1980s were the triumph of upper America—an ostentatious celebration of wealth, the political ascendancy of the rich and a glorification of capitalism, free markets and finance. Not only did the concentration of wealth quietly intensify, but the sums involved took a megaleap. The definition of who's rich—and who's no longer rich—changed as radically during the Reagan era as it did during the great nouveaux riches eras of the late 19th century and the 1920's, periods whose excesses preceded the great reformist upheavals of the Progressive era and the New Deal.

"But while money, greed and luxury became the stuff of popular culture, few people asked why such great wealth had concentrated at the top and whether this was the result of public policy. Political leaders, even those who professed to care about the armies of homeless sleeping on grates and other sad evidence of a polarized economy, had little to say about the Republican Party's historical role: to revitalize capitalism but also to tilt power, Government largess, more wealth and income toward the richest portion of the population." Kevin P. Phillips, *The New York Times Magazine*, Sunday, June 17, 1990. (For the full text of the article see Appendix 4.)

If the plutocracy controls the political process throughout the world; if the basic objective of the plutocracy is maximizing profit regardless of social consequences; if an adequate supply of cheap labor is an essential part of the profit-maximizing formula; and if the plutocracy is incapable of internalizing external costs, beyond perhaps the survival of its cheap labor base, then the choice facing humanity is either:

A. The extinction of a world that will support human beings
or
B. Reinstating: "Government of the **people**, by the **people** and for the **people**."

People engage in legitimate business activity for the purpose of making a profit. As long as the relationship between merchant and buyer, doctor and patient, craftsman and customer, remain one on one, human values can and do remain part of or even dominate the transaction. But as the process of organization develops, we begin to see companies, then corporations, and finally multi-national conglomerates. The larger and more diversified the business entity becomes, the further its management recedes from any form of human contact with other members of society, or consideration for the social consequences of their business decisions.

Decent, concerned people loving their families—good neighbors, charitable citizens—in their function as corporate managers put all of the above considerations aside as they become the servants of the profit-hungry institution they have created. Devoid of conscience and compassion, the business corporation is unable to perceive or understand that the common good is not synonymous with:

- maximizing profit
- market control and manipulation
- buying influence with elected officials
- in short, governing society for the benefit of the plutocracy and the impoverishment of all others

Not even the presence of the increasing destruction of the life-support capacity of this small planet seems to make it clear.

Fortunately, the Constitution and the system of government it established remains the law of the land. Now, we begin to see the wisdom of the men of 1787. In the voting booth the secret ballot of the multitude of **informed** citizens, voting their human concerns, outweighs the power of the plutocracy. The re-establishment of **real democracy** as outlined here is what Thomas Jefferson was talking about when he said, "The price of Liberty is Eternal Vigilance." To that we might add "and struggle." As the struggle to re-establish the control of government by all the people develops, we learn to build, not destroy. To create, not waste. To incorporate the needs of humanity within the ecosystem instead of functioning as an alien force destroying our own habitat.

As we change our ways, we begin to "change ourselves" and we learn new ways to live together. We talk about "human nature" as immutable, incorrigible and unmanageable. I have often wondered at the enormous range of human capacity. As a species we can range from saints to devils, from nurturers to murderers, from destroyers to creators. What Nancy Jack Todd is saying in her introduction means that the full range of the human potential exists in the genes of every baby from birth. We don't really have to change human nature; we have to learn to develop in ourselves the truly human capacities which separate us from the rest of life on this planet. Are we not talking about consciously moving the evolutionary process by building an environment for ourselves which will require the full play of these "truly human capacities" and reduce or eliminate the gain from exploitative behavior?

In so doing our America can finally fulfill its real destiny and become truly "the last best Hope of Earth."

Acknowledgements:

The Felix Rohatyn quotation was taken from an editorial in the June 1990 edition of the publication *Monthly Review*.

The James Madison quotations were taken from the book *Free Persons and the Common Good*, Michael Novak, Madison Books, 1989.

The H.J.M. de Vries quote was taken from his dissertation "Sustainable Resource Use," University of Groningen, Netherlands, 1989.

As this is written the crisis in the Middle East gives every indication of exploding into open warfare. Saddam Hussein is a power seeker in the age-old pattern of conquerors and oppressors. However, he has created mass support among the Arab peoples by pointing to Western exploitation of their only source of wealth . . . oil. Because of our hunger for oil we have become the allies of the Sheiks and Princes and the Kings of Arabia as the billions and billions of oil wealth are siphoned away from their people into overseas investments which in turn siphon wealth and jobs from American working people. That is Hussein's rallying cry and the source of his power.

If we were the stewards of Earth instead of its exploiters, the Husseins could not exist.

Managing the Transition

Again we refer to James Madison and the men of 1787:

"The interest of the man must be connected with the Constitutional rights of the place."

Consider that statement compared with: "Leave it all to the Market" or "Greed is Good" that the market has given us. Free market advocates want a form of *selective anarchy*. We are beginning to see the final implications of such a philosophy. Those who control the market (in our time the great transnational corporations of the developed world, Europe, North America, and Japan) want laws governing everybody and everything except their unrestricted right to make profits at the expense of all peoples everywhere, and now at the expense of all species of life on the entire planet.

According to economist Herman Daly, "Unless we awaken to the existence and *nearness* (sic) of scale limits, then the greenhouse effect, ozone layer depletion, and acid rain will be just a preview of disasters to come, not in the vague distant future, but in the next generation."

See Population And Development Review report of Hoover Institution Conference, paper by Herman E. Daly, Senior Economist, Environmental Division, World Bank. "SUSTAINABLE DEVELOPMENT: From Concept And Theory Towards Operational Principles." (Stanford, 2/1/89). From *State of the World 1990* we read, "If the world is to achieve sustainability, it will need to do so within the next 40 years. If we have not succeeded by then, environmental deterioration and economic decline are likely to be feeding on each other, pulling us into a downward spiral of social disintegration. Our vision of the future, therefore, looks to the year 2030."

See *State of the World 1990*, Chapter 10, page 174, Worldwatch Institute Report, Washington, D.C.

Those two somber statements tell us that the ever-increasing demands we have been placing upon the finite resources of our small planet have brought us to within a generation of the point of no return. What happens in this next decade is crucial, according to

Human Appropriation Of The Products of Photosynthesis, a Stanford University paper by Peter M. Vitousek and Associates (published in *Bio Science*, Volume 34, No. 6, May 1986, pages 368-373).

Photosynthesis is the almost miraculous process whereby plants and animals reciprocally use the direct energy of the sun to support all life on the planet. Plants create oxygen which all animals breathe, as well as food which we eat. We animals, on the other hand, create carbon dioxide which nourishes plant life. In short, photosynthesis is the process developed by nature over billions of years of time whereby life on earth converts the sun's radiant energy into the resources needed to support itself.

The Stanford study tells that in 1986 human activity was appropriating some 40 percent of the terrestrial photosynthetic capacity of the planet (i.e., oceans excluded as available only to humans through fisheries). The present rate of population increase is doubling the earth's population once every 40 years. As the rate of population increase is a growing figure, so is the rate at which humans are appropriating photosynthetic capacity. Starting with the current 40 percent appropriation and factoring in an increasing rate of population growth and an increasing rate of exploitation, a fairly firm consensus has emerged among scientists that beginning some 40 years from now we will have reached the point of no return.

We have come up with a target date to have in place, by the year 2000, the economic, the political and social programs for halting and reversing environmental degradation all over the planet, giving us the first 30 years of the next century to start stretching out the 40-year time table and build the basis for sustainable future. The functioning of a free society **presupposes** a level playing field, fair play, the team spirit. All these are universal American expressions of the fundamental proposition that civilized society means everybody plays by the same rules, **even the market**.

The statute books of every jurisdiction—local, state and federal—are filled with laws and regulations giving specific and overwhelming evidence that, as a people, we do consider that proposition to be the true meaning of America and not—"Money talks." Money has to talk in the interest of fair play for all or else the forty-year timetable to the beginning of social and economic disintegration will run its course and nature will have to go to work to develop a new species fit to care for the planet.

That is the new mindset, the mental leap which will free us to survive as a civilization.

The alternative is the dustbin of history.

* * *

The following is an outline of a ten-year program:

1. Develop and install economic efficiency measures
   a. In the appendix the reader will find the text of the testimony delivered before the California Energy Commission on June 18, 1990. In it we set forth a proposal to restructure motor vehicle liability insurance at annual savings to society of 50 to 60 billion dollars.
   b. In Chapter 7 Ted Flanigan (Energy Program Director, Rocky Mountain Institute, Snowmass, Colorado) details the saving of 300 billion dollars per year from increasing energy efficiency alone; without taking into account the new nonrenewable energy sources which are currently available. These are detailed by Bill Keepin in Chapter 6.

2. Develop and wage the campaign to recapture the political process:
   a. Starting with issues at the local level.
   b. Out of increasing voter registration, developing local candidates free of plutocratic control.
   c. Following these candidates to successively higher levels of political office until they are active throughout the land at all levels.
   d. Finance the campaign at $1 per month from tens of millions of concerned citizens, from public interest foundations and from members of the plutocracy who accept the need for change. Refer to Appendix 2 for a classic example of grassroots politics in action.

3. Monitor our candidates as the plutocracy attempts to co-opt them.

4. Use all this activity to create media events raising awareness and concern throughout the land.

5. Provide for the legitimate interests and welfare of all members of society through new jobs for old, for working people; retraining schools and living allowances for affected workers; investment and legitimate profit opportunities for affected industries; recalling our lawyers, our health providers, our accountants, our educators, and our journalists to true professional service and away from "profit at any cost."

6. As we begin to put our house in order, reach out to all the peoples of the world, helping them to do likewise in their own land in their own way. More on that in the appendix.

Chapters 5 through 11 of this volume tell of new technologies, new ways, new opportunities to restructure our civilization, to bring it into symbiotic harmony with the ecosystem which Earth, our mother, has created to support life for all her children. We must look to the new industries, the new orientations for old ones, which will produce new opportunities, new investments, new profits, new jobs and a *revitalized ecosystem for ourselves and our children.*

Anna Edey in Chapter 8 describes new techniques in agriculture which not only will solve food production problems, but call for investment and job opportunities involving millions of workers, in new, intensive, highly productive farming practices. She shows how food can be produced locally, instead of traveling an average of 1,300 miles to reach the consumer, saving energy and reducing cost, while increasing production. In this way food can be produced in harmony with the processes of nature. Two billion pounds annually of toxic pesticides will no longer contaminate our food and water. Whereas in the U.S., pesticide use has increased 1200% in the past thirty years, crop loss before harvest has doubled; large scale agribusiness is destroying the family farm, poisoning our land and wasting energy and raw materials. The illusion of plentiful food at low cost in the supermarket is just that—an illusion, now beginning to turn into the nightmare of unsustainable waste. Anna Edey teaches how to reclaim the deserts, renew irrigated lands, replace the topsoil, insure food for all humanity.

Combined with Anna Edey's new agriculture and solar energy (Bill Keepin, Chapter 6) present technology will allow the sun to desalinate sea water; provide nontoxic pure water to flush salt and chemicals from arable lands; provide energy to pump that pure water wherever needed; pasteurize all organic waste, eliminating the need for synthetic and toxic fertilizers; require entire new industries with profitable investments and new jobs worldwide.

As Dr. Keepin shows us, solar energy will also produce nonpolluting fuel (hydrogen) for public utilities; mass transportation; the new nonpolluting family car; required new industries, new investments, new jobs, new profits.

John Todd's "Living Machines," Chapter 9, tells us how to assemble natural organisms to produce fuel and food; treat waste; purify air; regulate climate; reduce the need for land fills; heat and cool buildings; protect and restore natural environment; turn sewage into drinking water.

Like Anna Edey, Dr. Todd turns to the mechanisms of the earth's own ecosystem to meet the needs of a truly advanced civilization living in harmony with its environment. Again, the opportunity for new investments, new jobs, new profits, new socially productive market opportunities.

Lastly we come to the "Lungs of the World," the great forests which produce the oxygen we humans need in return for the carbon dioxide we provide for them.

As we reclaim farmland, reduce waste and reclaim resources from our waste sites; the economic incentive to destroy the forests will be replaced with opportunity and land to reforest huge areas, to be carefully husbanded and cultivated for a world making constructive use of its land mass.

Deserts will gradually disappear as a feature of world geography.

Again new industries, new jobs, new profits, new markets worldwide.

Inertia overcome, we gain the momentum to implement a full program of political and social measures. Our relationship with the business community must continue to offer legitimate investment and profit opportunities. Additionally, the message has to come across that unless our business people can accept the need for long-term investments in the environment, encouraged by substantial tax incentives, then there will be no future in which to enjoy the short-term profits they are so busy grabbing these days. The historical record documents the use of tax initiatives to guide private risk/reward decisions along the path of agreed-upon public policy.

Most of the following suggestions were covered in hearings held by the House Ways and Means Committee March 6, 7, and 15, 1990.

During the coming decade we can incrementally:

1. Repeal the depletion allowance for petroleum-based fuels, and allow it doubly for end uses connected with the production of solar collecting installations, and the generation of power therefrom, and other ecologically benign end uses such as vessels for John Todd's living machines.

2. Place a tax on all petroleum imports to be used as fuel.

3. Provide for a graduated sales tax on all motor vehicles sold in the U.S. ranging from 100% on cars yielding less than 20 miles per gallon of gasoline to a negative figure of up to 50% (i.e., a government contribution or incentive) for the most economical vehicles yielding 90 mpg or better.

4. Place a pollution tax on all fuels and chemicals contributing to the degradation of the environment in direct proportion to their contribution to such degradation.

5. Phase out support for the nuclear energy industry entirely.

6. Place an additional excise tax on profits generated from mergers and acquisitions, at a level calculated to increase the speculative risk of such projects beyond acceptable risk/reward ratios.

7. Disallow the interest deduction on buyouts leveraged beyond a two to one debt to capital ratio.

8. Allow rapid depreciation and lower tax levels for investments in economic conversion industries.

9. Require holding an investment for five years to earn capital gain treatment.

10. Reverse the rules for the rate-making formulas of public utilities, to encourage investing in ecological retrofitting of customer facilities; and discouraging investment in new plants by keeping the

capital cost of such investments out of the formula, absent the use of nonpolluting fuels.

11. Make all federal grants to states and localities contingent upon their relative value in contributing to environmental recovery:

    a. Sewage disposal systems
    b. Waste management and recycling
    c. Cogeneration combustion of solid wastes
    d. Soil contamination and reclamation
    e. Ecological agriculture
    f. Ecology- and energy-efficient municipal planning and construction
    g. Reforestation.

12. Develop a policy for the ecological farming of our timberlands, and set tax policy for that industry accordingly; i.e., varying levels of taxation according to the practices of individual firms.

13. Carry the principle of variable taxation over to the enforcement area. In the present system, the fines for corporate violations of public policy in contract and performance areas generate barely a slap on the wrist for multi-billion dollar offenders.

However, a series of penalty tax brackets for such offenders might prove more effective, particularly if accompanied by restrictions on price increases during the penalty period.

Such a system would prevent a repeat of the *Valdez* experience, which the entire petroleum industry used as a pretext for raising prices during a period of excess supply.

14. Review and revise the student loan program to greatly expand retraining and orientation facilities for all workers leaving defense and polluting industries, as well as all workers seeking entrance into the labor market. This program to be coupled with tighter requirement of performance standards to correct present abuses.

15. Set up standards for contract awards by all public agencies, giving precedence to potential bidders in terms of their history of performance relative to the environment.

As this happens we are ready for the new human habitat described in Section IV by Richard Register and Kathryn McCamant. (Chapters 10 and 11)

In addition, the new educational system will need to train our young people for the new industries, for the new ways of living, and to prepare them to approach the peoples of the world using the new human ways.

Instead of military service we'll prepare our young people to spend a year or so between high school and college, to serve society here and abroad, to help create on this earth at last the truly human society encompassing all of God's creation.

Chapter 2

GRASSROOTS POLITICAL ACTION

by Nancy Skinner

A Call For Grassroots Democracy

Though most of us are familiar with the adage 'think globally and act locally,' too often we are unaware of the opportunities to effect significant change that are constantly available to us. The enormity of the environmental crisis gripping our globe makes it easy to feel helpless.

Daily we hear new reports of environmentally caused cancer clusters, are told on certain days not to exert ourselves or risk health damage from air pollution, or we read about the atmosphere's worsening ozone hole. Meanwhile, corporate leaders and government officials routinely deny the severity of the environmental crisis and act like everything's under control.

So, should we give up right now, stay depressed and stop reading? No. Our country's history has many examples of grassroots democracy in action. The American Revolution, the civil rights movement and the anti-war movement all demonstrate the powerful impetus for change that is mobilized when common people express their will.

We must take heart and remember that the strength of any society has always been its people. It's time we accept that government leaders and corporate decisionmakers are just humans like the rest of us—humans that have little more wisdom and ability to discern right from wrong and make decisions for the collective good than any other group of people. In other words, we have just as much expertise when it comes to what is good for our lives and the life of the planet as the next guy. And living in a democracy, I believe we have the responsibility to exercise our right to a healthy, sustainable environment whenever we feel that health is under threat.

Joanna Macy, a writer on subjects like living with hope in the nuclear age, talks about empowerment. "We need to recognize that denial itself is the greatest danger we face . . . the key is to not try to go it alone. Hook up with a group. Go to your church, your community center, your neighborhood school, find a group or start your own."[1] The founder of Friends of the Earth, David Brower, in his recent autobiography quotes Rene Dubos as saying "Trend is not destiny." Brower goes on to express: "If we keep following our present trend, we will indeed end up where we are headed. But that need not be our destiny. . . . Our best efforts should be aimed not at eroding the American Dream, but in restoring it."[2]

Unfortunately, the political and economic value systems that dominate most of the world's governments and corporations place a larger value on profits and staying in office than on preserving the health of people and the environment. These value systems have created a situation in which decisions by the politician are based on the size of the promised contribution and decisions by the corporation are based on the size of the expected profit.

We need the kind of grassroots action that can counteract the influence of big-bucks corporate campaign contributions. In the absence of an economic structure that builds in the true health and environmental costs of producing any given product, we need a level of political action that can compete with the influence of short-term profit motivation. Peter Montague, a member of the board of the Southwest Research and Information Center, advocates that "committed citizens . . . are the fire that will burn in the belly of Washington, helping Congress find the fortitude to pass tough laws."[3]

By and large, our educational systems and information media promote voting as the highest, and most acceptable, expression of public opinion and democratic participation. The message is if we all vote and we vote responsibly then our elected leaders will take care of everything and we won't have to worry—we can go back to watching our TV's! Of course it would help if more Americans, in fact, exercised their right to vote. More citizens voting would help

21

push government, on all levels, to become more accountable and more responsive to people's concerns. But, because the environmental crisis is at such an advanced stage, voting alone will not suffice. An additional expression of committment and activism from a significant number of people must reinforce any vote.

True democracy requires far more than voting. We must use the power of individual and grassroots collective action to express our will. One need only look at recent world events like the crumbling of the Berlin Wall and the South African government's negotiations with Nelson Mandela to realize this truth.

So how does all of this relate to our task of mending the earth? As Paul Rothkrug points out in the previous chapter, the time is short to achieve a system of sustainability. Even if each of as individuals were to practice the best conservation methods vis-à-vis our current resource use we would only be extending the ecological clock a small number of years. Creating a new *system* of sustainability is our fundamental challenge. Individual change alone will not be adequate. Yet, the critical element in winning this struggle is still individuals— committed individuals who join together to develop the blueprints for a sustainable system and then organize the community will necessary for its implementation.

The Flaws In The Federal Strategy

A look at the past helps explain why I believe grassroots political action and the building of a true environmental movement is necessary. The beginnings of the environmental movement in the 1970s were largely focused on developing federal legislation. A number of prominent environmental groups emerged, set up their headquarters in Washington D.C. and proceeded with what, at the time, seemed like a perfectly reasonable strategy. Ten major environmental laws were passed during the '70s and early '80s, e.g.: the National Environmental Policy Act, Clean Air Act, Clean Water Act, Toxics Substances Control Act, Resource Conservation and Recovery Act, etc. Barry Commoner describes this sequence of events eloquently in an article in the July 1987 issue of the *New Yorker*. Even though all of these laws were designed to clean up the environment, Commoner points out, since their passage there has been no substantive improvement in the quality of the U.S.'s air, water, soil or oceans.

The essential flaws in this strategy were: 1. The federal environmental regulations were designed to manage pollution once it was created. They did not attempt to get at the heart of why pollution was being created and what it would take to either reduce or eliminate that pollution. 2. The complex processes established by these laws gave an advantage to industry and large corporations through their ability to employ a vast array of legal and technical experts. These industry-hired experts became masters at arguing the standards, challenging the regulations, delaying the monitoring, and consequently eliminating enforcement, and 3. Citizens and environmental groups alike were lulled into a false sense of security, assuming that the myriad of federal regulations passed to protect and clean up the environment were in fact doing just that.

The Reasons For Local Action

The kind of change necessary to realize the sustainable system our future requires depends on the strength and breadth of grassroots political action. What will make the difference is the involvement of people—in huge numbers, from all walks of life, all classes, all races, all religions—standing up and speaking out for clean and healthy places to live and work.[4] Without the requisite people involvement expressed through grassroots organizing and action there is no environmental 'movement', and without an environmental movement there will not be the political will necessary to move us through the transition to sustainability.

Working on the local level—demanding action and organizing and developing policy—is the strategy I believe most likely to succeed in dealing with environmental problems for the following reasons:

1. To make an impact on the major global environmental problems—e.g. the greenhouse effect, resource depletion, ozone layer destruction—will require lifestyle changes and changes in the ways our entire society functions. The manner in which our current state and national governments operate ensures that they will be the last entities demanding this.

2. Most of our serious environmental problems are the result of the way we live in cities: the transportation systems, how the city is

designed, the resources consumed and how we consume them, the wastes we produce. The consequences of these problems often most directly affect the people living in the urban areas. People are most likely to respond when and where they are directly affected, and this is where change has to occur.

3. Because of the direct link to people in their communities, grassroots action and action by local governments have the greatest ability to educate and influence behavioral change.

4. Grassroots groups and citizen organizing involve a broader diversity of people. For example, coalitions battling the siting of hazardous waste facilities are rarely composed solely of people who are white, middle class, and/or view themselves as environmentalists. Often their involvement in the issue also addresses economic inequities and community degradation.

5. The reality is that major environmental battles over issues like landfilling and incineration vs. recycling and waste reduction or the siting of hazardous waste treatment facilities vs. toxics use reduction are being won and lost on the local level, not on the state and national level. The decisions resulting from these battles are what then influence government and corporate policy.

6. Local citizens and grassroots groups have a passion that's often lacking in state capitols or in Washington, because local citizens are fighting battles that directly affect their lives; they are not just fighting for abstract principles.

7. Local action and local legislation opens doors to what is politically possible in the larger arenas. It demonstrates that there is citizen or voter support and by doing so influences industry and corporate policies. Some of the most impressive state and federal environmental legislation enacted in the last few years e.g. mandatory recycling goals, hazardous materials disclosure or 'right to know' laws, were directly patterned after local government legislation and citizen initiatives.

8. Finally, grassroots organizing and citizen action provide a large-scale and effective citizen training ground. If we accept that we must maintain long-term education, organizing and life style changes in order to achieve sustainable development and a healthy environment, then citizens across this country and the globe will have to become part of a mass movement.[5]

Given the enormity of the task of making the transition to a life-sustaining system, achievement of the transition will depend on the existence of a broad-based grassroots environmental movement— one that is dedicated not only to restoring environmental quality but also to achieving environmental justice. Lois Gibbs, Executive Director of Citizens Clearinghouse for Hazardous Waste, is one of the foremost leaders of the grassroots movement for environmental justice in the U.S. As she writes in the Citizens Clearinghouse newsletter, *Everyone's Backyard,* "Environmental justice is broader than just preserving the environment. When we fight for environmental justice, we fight for our homes and families and struggle to end economic, social and political domination by the strong and greedy and the consequences it has on the world we live in."[6]

Examples of What You Can Do

Your own community, workplace, and local government provide a goldmine of opportunities for using grassroots political action to implement positive social change. Contrary to popular myth, you don't have to be in elected office to get local government to act or be the chairman of the board to change a business's policy. The following are some examples of citizens actions that not only effected change within their communities, but also served as a catalyst for change in much larger arenas.

Berkeley's 50% Recycling Goal

In the early 1970s, a group of citizens formed an ecology club and organized curbside recycling for the residents of the city of Berkeley, California. For years the Ecology Center ran the recycling program on a shoestring and as a mostly volunteer effort. But their fortitude paid off. The high level of citizen support for the program finally convinced the city government to give the Ecology Center a contract for their recycling activities.

Over the years people's enthusiasm for the Ecology Center's program grew. Other citizens began forming groups to develop additional recycling activities such as community composting, a buy-back center that paid people for the recyclables they brought, and a salvage yard to recover useable items like building materials, furniture, and appliances that otherwise would be thrown away. Before recycling became the popular household word it is today, a wide variety of citizen-initiated, community-sponsored recycling programs were available to Berkeley residents.

When Berkeley's landfill was scheduled to close, the city government was thrown into a panic. What were they going to do with all the garbage? Pleased with the recycling programs, citizen groups suggested that the city focus on expanding recycling as the number one waste management goal. Once that system was in place, the citizens suggested, the city could then determine what to do with whatever garbage was left. In 1980, this was an unheard-of proposition! City officials scoffed at the idea that you could recycle a significant amount of garbage. Instead, the public works department proposed that Berkeley become the first city in California to build a garbage incinerator, a 'modern' waste-to-energy plant, and eliminate some of the existing recycling programs.

Threatened with the possible closure of recycling programs, a number of citizen groups joined together to determine what could be done. They decided to write an initiative that would establish the goal of recycling 50% of Berkeley's waste. The necessary signatures were gathered to put the initiative on the ballot. In the 1984 election, Berkeley voters overwhelmingly passed the citizen-sponsored initiative, making Berkeley the first city in the country to set a 50% recycling goal. Various experts and the media ridiculed the plan and exclaimed "there goes Berserkley again!" Now, a short six years later, the California State legislature has passed a law requiring *every* city and county in the state to acheive 25% recycling and waste reduction by 1994, and 50% by the year 2000. Cities and states around the country are establishing similiar goals and calling for mandatory recycling.

Chain Reactions—Local Action as Catalyst

By establishing how the use of a certain product or material threatens the public good, cities have the power to enact bans. In Berkeley, we began talking about banning styrofoam to express our opposition to ozone-damaging CFCs as early as 1986. The ban was first recommended by the City's citizen Solid Waste Management Commission. Community groups like the Ecology Center, the Greens, groups committed to bayfront preservation and other waterfront issues, and businesses joined the effort and presented the issue to the City Council. Simply discussing the ban attracted national press. Shortly after, other organizations across the country began targeting McDonald's as a major user of CFC styrofoam, and they too received widespread press. Within six months, McDonald's Corporation and the polystyrene foam manufacturers announced their decision to eliminate the use of CFC as the blowing agent for polystyrene foam food packaging.

By the time the City Council passed Berkeley's styrofoam ban in 1988, CFCs were no longer the primary issue. Styrofoam became a symbol of wasteful, environmentally damaging packaging and of the United State's phenomenal garbage crisis. Cities across the country followed Berkeley's lead and laws quickly passed in Portland, Oregon; Minneapolis, Minnesota and Newark, New Jersey. Now over 100 local governments have passed laws, some even stronger and more comprehensive than Berkeley's, and the plastics industry is scrambling to develop and promote recyclable plastics.[7]

Power to the People in Minnesota

In order to strengthen their community and political effectiveness, citizens in Minnesota formed a coalition of 22 existing organizations representing a broad range of issues including: the environment, peace, human rights and economic and social justice. Named the Minnesota Alliance for Progressive Action (MAPA), the coalition's purpose is to organize people around these issues, to increase participation in the democratic process and to bring about systemic change.

Formed less than four years ago, MAPA has made tremendous accomplishments in increasing voter registration and voter turn out. Providing coalition members and other citizens opportunities for education and training is an explicit and conscious strategy of MAPA. They regularly hold campaign trainings for volunteers, potential candidates, and campaign organizers and sponsor community conferences on issues such as building progressive power in the legislature and using electoral strategies to empower the community. Rather than relying on the usual political 'old boys school' to generate candidates for public office, MAPA is now beginning to run candidates from their member groups for city and statewide positions.[8]

Church Members as Stewards of the Earth

Wanting to recycle rather than throw good resources away and frustrated by local government's inaction, Vision, a church-based group in Alabama, took matters into their own hands by setting up recycling centers at churches throughout their county. "The Earth is the Lord's" is the subheading of their newsletter, *The Perspective*. The pages are filled with stories from churches whose congregations were successful in halting toxic waste incineration, stopping the filling of nearby wetlands or cleaning up polluted streams.[9]

Union Members and Neighbors Form 'Toxic Waste Squad'

Auddie Shelby is a United Auto Workers member from Sumpter Township, Michigan. As the UAW's Earth Day '90 pamphlet tells it, "Not too long ago, Auddie spent more time organizing his fishing tackle than organizing protests against toxic waste."[10] Learning of proposals to build a toxic waste dump and incinerator on a marsh near his home, Auddie got other members of his local union to form a 'Toxic Waste Squad'. In two weeks they had collected 400 signatures opposing the dump; then Auddie went to other local unions for support. The Squad was successful and the dump plans were shelved.

Since that time, the Squad has co-sponsored legislation to strengthen toxic waste laws, joined with local high school students to eliminate styrofoam trays from their school cafeteria, and promoted recycling in nearby towns. Shelby believes that people "have a right to our voices and our destiny," and he is proud that his group acted on those beliefs. "If we can join together, and make a difference in the future quality of our grandchildren's lives," says Shelby, "anyone can."[11]

The Pen is Mightier Than the Sword

Maybe some of you are not yet ready to join a group or form one of your own. Don't worry, there are still avenues available to you for political activism. Utilizing the power of the written word through letter writing and petitions remains an effective expression of grassroots democracy. There are a number of organizations designed to make it easy for people to use their pens to make a difference. A group called Global Action Network sends out "Action Requests," informative reports with petitions or letters which need to be written on a particular subject. Each report provides background information, the suggested action to take, and results from previous efforts.[12] Another group, 20/20 Vision, will send their subscribers a monthly postcard spelling out the most important letters they can write in a single 20-minute stretch of time to further the goals of world peace and global security.[13]

Whatever actions you choose to take or organizations you choose to join, the key is to do it and do it now. I hope these simple examples inspire you to take up the challenge of helping move our planet and life on earth through the transition to a sustainable future. There is no more potent force that can be brought to bear on acheiving this goal than our own.

References

1. Joanna Macy, *In Context* Magazine, Number 22, titled: "Global Climate Change—Social and Personal Responses," Editor: Robert Gilman.

2. David R. Brower, *The Life and Times of David Brower.* 1990, published by Gibbs Smith, Salt Lake City.

3. Peter Montague, "What We Must Do—A Grassroots Offensive Against Toxics in the '90s," The Workbook, July/September 1989, published by the Southwest Research and Information Center, Albuquerque, New Mexico.

4. Lois Gibbs, Editor's Comments, *Everyone's Backyard,* Volume 8, Number 1, January-February 1990. Published by Citizen's Clearinghouse for Hazardous Waste, Inc., Arlington, Virginia.

5. I am indebted to Peter Montague's article referred to above and Alan B. Durning's article "Grassroots Groups Are Our Best Hope for Global Prosperity and Ecology" which appeared in the July/August 1989 issue of the *Utne Reader.*

6. Lois Gibbs, *ibid.*

7. For more information on cities with plastics and packaging reduction laws and other communities' innovative environmental

programs, contact Local Solutions to Global Pollution, 2121 Bonar St., Studio A, Berkeley, California 94702.

8. Minnesota Alliance for Progressive Action, 1929 South Fifth Street, Minneapolis, Minnesota 55454.

9. *The Perspective*, published by Vision, P.O. Box 217, Montevallo, Alabama 35115.

10. Penelope Whitney, "The Earth and Us—UAW Members Show How to Change The World As Earth Day Nears." *Solidarity*, March 1990, published by the United Auto Workers.

11. Penelope Whitney, *ibid.*

12. Global Action Network c/o Earthright Institute, Gates-Briggs Building, Room 322, White River Junction, Vermont 05055.

13. 20/20 Vision, 1181-C Solano Ave., Albany, California 94706.

Chapter 3

GREEN SEALS
Harnessing Market Forces to Protect the Earth

by Denis Hayes

Introduction

According to a 1989 *New York Times*/CBS News poll, an astonishing 80 percent of all Americans believe that "protecting the environment is so important that requirements and standards cannot be too high, and continuing environmental improvements must be made regardless of cost." Even allowing for the error margins inherent in opinion sampling, this is an extraordinary expression of support for such a strong formulation of the primacy of environmental values over narrower economic interests.

Adding significance to the 1989 poll results is that they fall in line with a decade-long trend. When *The New York Times* first asked this question in a 1981 poll, just 45 percent agreed. Agreement with the proposition has increased regularly with each subsequent polling— even in the environmental dog days of James Watt and Anne Gorsuch.

People are manifesting their concern for the environment in myriad ways. Increasingly, environmental issues influence politics, law, education, religion, investments, and lifestyles. One of the most intriguing demonstrations of rising environmental consciousness is in consumer behavior.

A 1989 market survey performed for the Michael Peters Group— a leading international consulting firm specializing in new product design—found that 89 percent of Americans express concern over the impact that their purchases make on the environment, and more than half claim to have refused to buy an item because of the environmental harm it caused.

A consumer boycott of aerosol propellants in the late 1970s led to a federal ban on the use of ozone-depleting chlorofluorocarbons (CFCs) as propellants. A consumer boycott of the nation's tuna canning companies in 1989-90 arguably did more to protect dolphins than had the previous two decades of environmental lobbying in Washington, D.C.

Moreover, boycotts are now being joined by positive "buycotts," as increasing numbers of consumers patronize manufacturers that are viewed as friendly toward the environment. Environmentally-sensitive consumers have propelled such young companies as the Body Shop, Esprit, Aveda, Ben and Jerry's, and Tom's of Maine into some of the most successful enterprises of the 1980s.

According to a national survey conducted last year for *Advertising Age* by the Gallup Organization, 96% of women and 92% of men would make a special effort to buy products from companies trying to protect the environment; 90% of women and 87% of men indicated that they would be willing to pay more for products or packaging that are environmentally safer. According to the journal *American Demographics*, environmentally-sensitive consumption "is a bigger market than some of the hottest markets of the '80s."

Many manufacturers and retailers are seeking ways to capitalize on public concern for the environment, with varying degrees of opportunism and cynicism. Some of the resulting claims for the environmental merits of products appear to be designed to mislead consumers. Insupportable claims have been made for products ranging from biodegradable plastics to water purifiers. Minnesota's Attorney General, Hubert H. Humphrey, III, has predicted that "the selling of the environment . . . will become the next great consumer battleground." Mr. Humphrey, joined by several other attorneys general, recently attacked major manufacturers of "biodegradable" trash bags for misleading the public.

Consumer-driven concern for the environment could be undermined if people were to change their habits or pay a premium to buy what they though was an environmentally superior product—only to later learn that they had been misled.

Indeed, an alarming level of skepticism has already developed—doubtless rooted in empty claims that products are degradable, biodegradable, photodegradable, natural, recycled, recyclable, environment friendly, earth friendly, ozone friendly, etc.

Most such claims are themselves "photodegradable": they disintegrate when exposed to light. For example, describing something as "degradable" merely admits that it is subject to the Second Law of Thermodynamics.

Seven out of ten American adults now dismiss the environmental claims of most manufacturers as hype. They want some independent body that they can trust to give them the truth about which soaps, paints, light bulbs, refrigerators, and other consumer products are doing an exceptional job of protecting and enhancing the environment.

A 1990 poll conducted by Research and Forecasts found that 80 percent of the public would be inclined to rely upon an environmental label affixed to a product if the label were awarded by an independent group whose competence and integrity were beyond question. That is the mission of the Green Seal.

Goals and Rationale

Twenty years after the first Earth Day in 1970, the environmental movement has fallen far short of its goals. Measured on virtually any scale, the world is in much worse shape today than it was two decades ago.

The reasons for this are complex. An important part of the explanation is that American environmentalists have been preoccupied with government as an instrument of change. We discounted the importance of economic choices and personal behavior, and put all our effort into winning elections, lobbying politicians, and filing lawsuits.

This was a strategic mistake for two reasons:

First, people have enormous power to promote rapid change by business when they send clear signals through the market. No company wants to lose market share.

Second, the choices made by millions of consumers have vast direct impacts on the environment. The used motor oil improperly disposed of last year by individual Americans was eleven times as great as that spilled by the Exxon *Valdez*.

A group of environmentalists, consumer activists, and other leaders recently formed a new non-profit group—Green Seal—to educate consumers about the consequences of their choices. Green Seal's board includes the Chairman of the Sierra Club, the President of the Worldwatch Institute, and the Executive Directors of the Natural Resources Defense Council, the Environmental Defense Fund, and the Rainforest Action Network. Its consumer representatives include Esther Peterson, Special Assistant for Consumer Affairs to Presidents Johnson & Carter and the C.E.O.'s of the Council on Economic Priorities and of the U.S. Public Interest Research Group.

Among the many other distinguished directors are Hubert H. Humphrey, III, Attorney General of Minnesota; Reverend Joseph Lowery, President of the Southern Christian Leadership Conference; Alan Kay, President of On Line Markets; and Jan Hartke, Vice President of the Humane Society.

The goal of Green Seal is to use market forces to help create a world that is healthy, diverse, and sustainable. Toward that end, Green Seal is creating an environmental certification program for consumer products. This program will award a readily identifiable label to products that, from cradle to grave, are environmentally acceptable.

Drawing on the Experience of Others

Late 1970s, the United Nations Environmental Program suggested that countries set up environmental labeling programs as one means of educating consumers. Initially, only Germany picked up the idea. However, in recent years several other countries have followed suit.

Green Seal has studied the numerous other environmental labeling program around the world. That study documented the enormous potential of green labeling, and it helped identify possible pitfalls that Green Seal must avoid.

Today, the major environmental labeling programs in the world include:

West Germany. The Federal Republic of Germany established the first environmental labeling program in 1977. The program involves both governmental and non-governmental decision-making bodies. The program is governed by an independent Jury, and managed by the private German Institute for Quality Assurance and Labeling. Criteria are set by experts drawn from industry, consumer groups, environmental groups, and others. The Federal Environmental Agency finally takes part in an advisory, but a very influential, capacity.

The West German program's logo is called the "Blue Angel." It is the United Nations logo of a blue figurine inside a circle of grain. The Blue Angel has now been awarded to over 3300 products in 58 product categories. About 200 suggestions for new product categories are received by the program each year. More than 10 percent of the companies awarded the label are foreign.

A 1987 survey found that 70 percent of German households were familiar with the Blue Angel. Moreover the criteria for the Blue Angel are usually adopted by all levels of government in the specifications for governmental procurement.

Although the German program aspires to encompass the myriad impacts caused by a product through its entire life cycle, in practice the German criteria are sometimes limited to a single factor. For example, certain gasoline-powered lawn mowers are eligible for the seal based solely on their noise levels—without reference to the fact that hand-pushed lawn mowers make even less noise and also consume no fossil fuels.

This single criterion approach has been criticized as overly simplistic. The West German program has also been criticized for allowing its product criteria to become outdated.

Despite these limitations, the West German program is having a positive impact on the environment. For example, according to one recent study the program has had a significant impact on paper manufacturers' investments in new plants, changes in production practices, and development of improved products. The Blue Angel's managers estimate that their seal has resulted in a 30 percent reduction in average emissions from oil and gas heaters, and a cumulative reduction of 40,000 tons of organic solvents from household paints reaching the waste stream. Today, Blue Angel-approved paints have a 30 percent market share, compared with just 5 percent before the program began.

Canada. The Canadian labeling program, "Environmental Choice," is only three years old. The Canadian effort, while retaining a private dimension, is more dominated by the government than the German program. The Minister of the Environment is responsible for the program under the law, and the program's staff are employees of Environment Canada (the federal environmental agency). Although the program is governed by an volunteer board that is technically "independent," the board and its chairman are selected by the Environment Minister. Moreover, the Environment Minister must approve all the Environmental Choice guidelines before their final issuance.

The Canadian program's "EcoLogo" symbol is a maple leaf composed of three doves—symbolizing consumers, business and government all working in unison.

Guidelines for ten Canadian product categories have now been established, including re-refined oil, a construction material consisting of recycled wood fiber, recycled plastic products, zinc-air batteries, fine paper from recycled paper, newsprint from recycled paper, miscellaneous products from recycled paper, water-based paints, cloth diapers, and heat recovery ventilators. Draft guidelines have been prepared for energy-efficient major appliances, reusable shopping bags, sanitary paper from recycled paper, composting units, gasohol, and reusable shopping bags.

Canada's Environmental Choice program attempts to use a multiple-criteria, cradle-to-grave approach. Initially the Canadians planned to use a matrix that awarded points to each candidate product based on its environmental acceptability at each stage of its life cycle. That approach proved too rigid, however, and it has been abandoned in favor of a more flexible ad hoc method.

One criticism of the Canadian program is that it took too long (almost 3 years) to establish its initial criteria. However, if given a choice between a very slow (but fairly well-considered) program like Canada's, or a much more speedy (but also more superficial) program like Japan's, most environmentalists would vote for Canada's approach.

In the final analysis, Canada's program has not been in place long enough to allow an informed judgment of its impact. A recent independent report notes that the response to date from most consumers and most industrial participants has been positive. Nevertheless, some environmental critics argue that the criteria are too slack and that pedestrian products are being awarded the seal. Other critics have claimed to see evidence of political influence.

Japan. In February, 1988, Japan's Environment Association, under the direction of the country's Environment Agency, began a labeling program known as "Eco-Mark." Japan's effort is a modified version of the West German program. The program uses a label that contains the letter "e," shaped into arms and hands, cradling the earth.

Japan launched its labeling effort with aerosol products using non-CFC propellants; kitchen strainers; sink filters; composters for organic wastes; used cooking oil bags, and books and magazines from recycled paper. From seven categories in February, 1988, the program has now expanded to cover 22 categories, including *inter alia* toilet paper, soap, recycled plastics, recycled paper products, and solar energy systems. An amazing 441 individual products already had been licensed to use the Eco-Mark by May, 1990.

The Japanese program awards its Eco-Mark to products that purportedly cause little or no pollution in use, improve the environment during use, cause little or no pollution when discarded, and otherwise contribute to the conservation of the environment. Attention ostensibly is paid to the environmental impact of manufacturing processes, to compliance with all applicable laws, and to competitive price.

Some critics voice concern over the superficial analysis behind some of the Japanese product choices, and also over the Eco-Mark's early emphasis upon product categories with trivial environmental consequences (e.g. sink filters, kitchen strainers, sponges, and "cans with stay-on tabs"). Supporters argue that Japanese consumers have not yet experienced the surge of environmental awareness that gripped other industrial countries in the 1980s, and that the Eco-Mark is intended to be only a very modest first step toward heightened environmental awareness.

Other Programs Outside the U.S. Several other countries are planning or discussing environmental labeling programs. Norway is developing a labeling effort using a new, independent non-profit foundation. A government commission in Sweden has proposed a green labeling effort. All the Scandinavian countries have considered using a common symbol and a common set of labeling criteria.

Independent programs are currently under development in France, the Netherlands, Great Britain, and Spain. In addition, the European Commission is investigating a possible labeling program for the European Economic Community, to begin in 1992 with the greater European integration.

Environmental Labeling Initiatives in the United States

Federal Labeling Activity. Compared to other countries, there has been little activity in the U.S. federal government to implement an environmental labeling program. In 1989, the U.S. Environmental Protection Agency commissioned a report from a consulting firm—Applied Decisions Analysis—on the possibility of a U.S. environmental labeling program. The ADA report recommends creation of an independent, non-profit organization very similar to the foundation that runs the Norwegian program, rather than placing such an effort inside a federal agency.

Various EPA offices, including the air and solid waste programs, have commissioned studies and other work that may be relevant to a possible U.S. labeling program, including research into life cycle product analysis and package labeling to reduce waste.

Some members of Congress have proposed legislation to label packaging and/or products. However, passage of comprehensive environmental labeling legislation by Congress seems highly unlikely. Representatives of several large national environmental organizations have argued strongly that a private effort would be preferable to a governmental program. Congress is unlikely to establish a federal environmental labeling program opposed by the environmental movement. Moreover, both Congress and the President are reluctant to undertake any new programs during this time of soaring budget deficits.

Absent new legislation, no current federal agency has the power to begin a broad environmental product labeling effort. However, the Federal Trade Commission and an eight-state task force are discussing possible ways to regulate labels to prevent misleading claims. At the present time, such guidelines appear likely to focus only on product waste and not the overall environmental impact of the product being labeled.

State proposals. Most state activity to date has focussed on reducing waste by labeling product packaging. New York has a law regulating the labeling of products as "recycled," "recyclable" or "reusable." Rhode Island recently proposed labeling rules for recycled products. The state of Washington has passed legislation creating a task force to develop a labeling program for packaging. Illinois and Minnesota have debated legislative proposals on labeling packaging. And the Northeast Governors are working jointly with the Northeast Recycling Council on an initiative that would regulate the labeling of materials used in packaging.

Private labeling initiatives. Several retail chains including Wal-Mart Stores, Safeway, Giant and Loblaw either have adopted their own environmental labeling programs or have set aside aisles to call attention to products whose manufacturers make environmental claims for them. Most of these chains do no independent verification of manufacturers' claims. Four western supermarket chains, including Ralphs Grocery and Payless, have announced an intention to work cooperatively to encourage environmentally sensitive consumption. Scientific Certification Systems, an organization that certifies pesticide-free products, has announced plans to eventually issue a "green cross" seal to certain non-food products.

Already, some of these private sector initiatives have been criticized in the news media as contributing to a proliferation of separate and potentially confusing labels. Moreover, retailers' claims are under the same cloud of suspicion by consumers as are manufacturers' claims, since both have a vested interest in increasing sales. One national environmental group is considering a major campaign against misleading environmental claims—"greenwash"—by retail chains.

Lessons from Non-Environmental Labels

The United States has a wealth of experience to draw upon in private certification programs for other than environmental features. Among such programs are the well-known seal for kosher foods, the Underwriter's Laboratory Seal, the Good Housekeeping Seal, and the American Dental Association seal. The experience of all these programs will be invaluable to the environmental labeling field in areas ranging from quality assurance to public education. Additionally, all share a need to maintain a very high degree of public credibility.

One recent ill-fated labeling program is worthy of special mention. The American Heart Association recently canceled its proposed "Heart Guide" program to label foods that met certain low-fat, low-salt guidelines. The AHA program had encountered extensive criticism for refusing to release data on the precise nutritional requirements that its endorsed products were supposed to meet. Advisors had cautioned that these criteria should not be disclosed for proprietary reasons, but the result was a public relations disaster. AHA also was criticized for certifying foods that critics claimed were not "healthy" such as margarine, cooking oil, and crackers. Other critics were upset by the high fees that the AHA proposed to charge companies—fees that critics claimed would discriminate against smaller companies. The final straw came when the federal Food and Drug Administration announced that it intended to create its own competing health labeling program, and that it might seize products bearing the AHA label.

Green Seal will avoid these problems by taking several steps. First, in sharp contrast to the Heart Guide program, Green Seal will make its criteria open to the public. Indeed, Green Seal will encourage extensive public involvement in the standard-setting process. Second, Green Seal will not certify categories that create environmental destruction without proportionate social utility, nor will it certify individual products unless they possess significant environmental advantages over their competitors. Third, Green Seal will charge reasonable fees. It guarantees that no qualifying product will ever be denied a seal because a manufacturer cannot afford the testing fees. Finally, at least for the time being, Green Seal will not evaluate food products, pharmaceutical products, or other products that might put it into conflict with labeling programs conducted by the federal government.

The American "Green Seal"

The need has emerged for an authoritative non-profit national environmental certification program to cut through the cacophony and provide consumers with a source of trustworthy information about environmentally acceptable products. Key leaders in the environmental movement, together with a broad cross-section of others whose integrity is beyond reproach, have committed themselves to creating such a Green Seal.

For several months, the staff of Green Seal has been studying environmental labeling programs around the world. It has engaged in wide-ranging consultations with key certification experts in the United States, including Underwriters Laboratory, Consumers Union, and the Good Housekeeping Institute. Having sought to learn from the successes and mistakes of others, Green Seal now is embarking upon an ambitious effort to establish a *de facto* national standard.

In general terms, the decision-making process for the U.S. Green Seal will proceed as follows:

1. Selection of product categories

On a regular basis, Green Seal will issue a public call for nominations of categories of consumer products to be considered for the seal. Manufacturers, trade associations, environmental and consumer groups, and government officials will be contacted directly and asked for their assistance. From this public input, the Green Seal board of directors will decide which categories should be assigned the highest priority for evaluation.

In weighing which categories to select, the board will consider recent innovations in product design or manufacturing processes that may constitute an environmental "breakthrough." Other important factors include the overall significance for the environment of each proposed category, and the likelihood that consumer decisions about each category will be strongly influenced by environmental considerations.

After consulting with several dozen organizations, the Green Seal decided to focus upon the following product categories for its first seal candidates:

- Light Bulbs
- Laundry Products
- Household Paint
- Toilet Paper
- Facial Tissues

Other candidates for early consideration include:

- Home Cleansers
- Low-Flow Shower Heads
- Batteries
- Office Paper
- Recycled Motor Oil
- Shampoo
- Retreaded tires
- Bicycles

2. Development of proposed product criteria

Green Seal's staff will contact manufacturers of products in each category chosen for inclusion in the Green Seal program. Similarly, the staff will approach public interest organizations, scientists, trade associations, and government officials to solicit recommendations about the appropriate environmental criteria for each category. The criteria may cover any and all stages in the product's life cycle, from the mining of its raw materials to its eventual recycling or disposal.

The goal of Green Seal is to improve the quality of the Earth's environment by educating consumers about the consequences of their choices. It will promote the following objectives:

- **Toxic and Radioactive Chemical Pollution.** Reduce the volume and toxicity of chemicals being released into the environment. Eliminate immediately the release of chemicals known or suspected to cause cancer, mutations, birth defects, and other serious threats to human health. Dramatically reduce and make progress toward eliminating the release of all other persistent hazardous chemicals.

• **Energy Use.** Significantly reduce the use of fossil and nuclear fuels by maximizing the efficiency of energy use, and by employing renewable energy sources, in the manufacturing process and to power the product itself.

• **Water Supplies.** Protect the quality and quantity of water resources by increasing the efficiency of water use, dramatically reducing pollution of surface and groundwater supplies, protecting wetlands, improving water supply management, and assuring sufficient flows of water for indigenous waterlife.

• **Wild Living Resources.** Treat the earth's living resources with respect and encourage biological diversity by maintaining and restoring natural plant and animal habitats, preventing the extinction of species, and eliminating the unnecessary use of animal testing.

• **Natural Areas.** Halt the damage or loss of the world's natural areas, including its forests, wetlands, parks, ranges and refuges.

• **Material Resources.** Eliminate the waste of natural resources by reducing the use of materials, making maximum use of recycled materials, and producing products that are durable, repairable, and designed to facilitate the recycling of their components at the ends of their useful lives.

• **The Atmosphere.** Reduce the release of chemicals that contribute to global warming or acid rain, and eliminate chemicals that cause significant damage to the Earth's protective ozone shield.

Final decisions on criteria will be made by Green Seal's "Environmental Standards Council." The Council will be composed of independent scientists and other experts qualified to evaluate environmentally-based standards for consumer products.

The members selected for the Environmental Standards Council will be of unquestioned competence and integrity. The Standards Council, like the Green Seal board of directors and the staff, will operate under a strict Code of Ethics assuring that no person can influence a labeling decision in which he or she has a financial interest.

3. Public review of proposed product criteria

Once proposed criteria have been established, they will be published—along with their rationale—for review by the public.

Green Seal will make a special effort to reach out to the affected industry, to labor, to governmental regulators, and to environmental and consumer interests. Green Seal will accept written comments on the proposed criteria. In the case of especially important or controversial criteria, it may hold public hearings on them.

4. Final approval

Following the public review period, Green Seal's staff will analyze the public comments received and propose any appropriate changes in the criteria. The Environmental Standards Council will make the final decision as to product criteria. The final criteria will be sent to manufacturers of products in the category, to those who commented on the proposed product criteria, and to other interested persons.

In addition to criteria related to specific product categories, Green Seal will also establish generic criteria applicable to all products. For example, manufacturers will be required to prove that their products are manufactured in accordance with all applicable environmental laws and regulations.

5. Product Testing and Certification

Once criteria have been established, any company that believes it sells a product meeting those criteria may apply to Green Seal for a license to use the seal on packaging and in advertisements. A research and testing fee will be established at a level to cover all expected expenses of research and testing of the product. Small manufacturers for whom the standard testing fee would be a hardship will be given special consideration. **No product that meets the Green Seal criteria will ever be denied a seal because its manufacturer could not afford the testing fees.**

Initially, all testing will be conducted by qualified independent testing laboratories using the final product criteria. Green Seal has explored relationships with several such laboratories, and it has several attractive opportunities.

Green Seal will determine whether a product meets the Green Seal criteria, as reflected in the results from independent testing laboratories as well as research into the product's manufacturing and disposal. Such research will be conducted by Green Seal staff, the

Environmental Data Bank of the Council on Economic Priorities, Franklin Research and Development, other contractors, and upon verified data presented by the company or by government agencies.

Any company aggrieved by the denial of a Green Seal to one of its products may appeal that decision to the Environmental Standards Council.

Green Seal will make no disclosure of the names of products or companies that fail to meet the criteria, unless such disclosure is required to defend Green Seal itself from legal actions or damaging public attacks.

6. Granting the Green Seal

All products that meet or exceed the Green Seal criteria will be eligible to use the mark. Licenses will be issued to such products for an initial period of no more than three years. The license agreements will provide, among other things, that the company must continue to meet or exceed the established product criteria.

Green Seal will monitor each licensee's compliance with the Green Seal criteria. This monitoring may include random testing of products, site visit to manufacturing facilities, examination of government regulatory records, and such other actions as may be needed to assure that the integrity of the Green Seal is preserved.

In the event that a brand fails to adhere to the Green Seal criteria, Green Seal will take whatever actions are necessary to remove the seal from non-qualifying merchandise.

7. Reconsideration of product criteria

The environmental criteria established for each product category will be reviewed at least once every three years. Where appropriate, new criteria will be proposed and a new public comment period held. The purpose behind this periodic review of product criteria is to aggressively encourage and reward innovation, as well as to incorporate any new information on environmental impacts.

The process described above should be viewed as a first step in an evolving effort to design a flexible but highly effective environmental labeling program. It attempts to accommodate the need for rigorous standards with a need to respond swiftly to important technological innovations. The process may be altered as Green Seal acquires more experience and as creative suggestions are received from the public, industry, environmental experts, and others.

Public Education

Green Seal is an entirely voluntary program. It will succeed only if qualifying companies decide to use the Green Seal on their products and if consumers switch their buying preferences to those products. To encourage support for its label, Green Seal will develop a major public education campaign that will include, among other things:

• **Marketing Strategy**

Green Seal will develop a strategy for marketing itself to consumers and industry. The strategy will include market research to identify factors that will increase consumer and industry acceptance of the Green Seal process. Among other things, Green Seal will conduct public opinion polls to gauge consumer reaction to its work, and will develop strategies to improve public acceptance of the Green Seal. The first such poll was recently completed for Green Seal by Research and Forecasts, Inc.

• **Public Service Advertising**

Green Seal will use television, radio and print public service advertising to explain the meaning of the Seal and to encourage consumers to use it in selecting products to purchase.

• **Educational Material**

Green Seal will prepare and distribute a variety of publications, including colorful and easily readable pamphlets and brochures, describing the criteria for each category, explaining how products obtain the Seal, and listing the products to have received Seals to date. Other materials will explain the impact of a single consumer purchasing and using each certified product, and the aggregate impact of the whole society doing so. We will attempt to make the materials available to consumers in supermarkets, department stores, popular media, and other locations where it is likely to have an impact.

Green Seal will approve written descriptions of the certified environmental benefits of each product which manufactures can use in advertisements and on packaging for qualifying products. Additionally, Green Seal will employ PSAs, audio-visual materials, and other materials to educate the general public about the generic meaning and value of the Green Seal.

• Catalog of Tested Products

Green Seal will regularly publish a popularly written description of the criteria for each consumer product category, a list of qualifying products that were tested, and an explanation of the environmental benefits gained by using products bearing the Green Seal.

What Green Seals Cannot Do

Green consumer organizing may be the most powerful new environmental force to emerge in the last decade. However, it has important limits. It is a supplement to other forms of environmental activism, not a substitute for them.

Green consumption is still consumption. When the goal is to stop consumer use of a whole class of unnecessary products—such as electric can openers—or to reduce the amount of consumption of goods in whole categories—such as fossil fuels—a Green Seal will be of little help.

Moreover, there are myriad problems for which consumer action is not an effective instrument. Consumer power will have little effect upon toxic dumps at military bases. Consumers cannot stop a freeway or build a public transportation system. Consumers will not safeguard national parks; promote sustainable agriculture in the Horn of Africa; or procure such large volumes of costly solar cells that prices will fall dramatically due to efficiencies of scale. All these, and thousands of other environmental objectives can be achieved only through traditional environmental activism.

Still, the remaining roles for consumerism in shaping the environment is formidable. It is of enormous importance that the job be done well. Irreversible thresholds may be crossed during the next decade unless we begin immediately to change our behavior. We don't have time to keep making mistakes.

Conclusion

Political change is often slow and ineffective. The Clean Air Act of 1990 was the target of a ten-year fight on Capitol Hill, and the final product is deeply compromised. More years of regulatory rule-making lie ahead. Then enforcement officials will be under great pressure to compromise or delay its implementation. Companies can sometimes afford to support battalions of lobbyists, defend lengthy lawsuits, or even pay large fines. Delay equals money in the bank.

But no company can afford to hemorrhage market share. If the Green Seal gives environmentally superior brands a meaningful advantage in the marketplace, competitors must respond immediately—doing whatever is necessary in order to win a Green Seal for their own products.

Chapter 4

ECOLOGICAL ECONOMICS
A new approach to understanding and managing the interactions of humans and nature.
by Robert Costanza and Lisa Wainger

Is a swamp worth more than a shopping mall? Perhaps not, at first blush. But what if we discover that the swamp is cleaning sewage and trapping atmospheric carbon? Does its "value" increase? If so, by how much? How many such valuable services does it take for the swamp to be worth more than the shopping mall?

Answers to questions like these may be hard to come by, but we've been making things more difficult than we have to. By viewing ecological problems as a battle between economic interests and environmental interests, we force groups to take sides to their own (and society's) mutual detriment. But what if environmental interests could be incorporated into economic planning? What if environmental assets were routinely considered in our economic accounting system? Could economic forces then be used to preserve the environment?

If we are ever to find workable long-term solutions to our environmental problems, we need a completely new conception of the relationship between economics and ecology, one that regards the economic subsystem as a part of the larger ecological life-support system. Such a conception must go beyond the narrow boundaries of the traditional academic disciplines to extend and integrate the study and management of "nature's household" (ecology) and "humankind's household" (economics). It must acknowledge that in the long run a healthy economy can only exist in symbiosis with a healthy ecology.

Ecological economics is beginning to be put into practice by a recently formed worldwide, multidisciplinary group called the International Society for Ecological Economics. They are in the forefront of a growing realization: that the most obvious danger of excluding nature from economics is that nature is the economy's life-support system, and that by ignoring it we may inadvertently damage it beyond repair. Current economic systems do not have built-in methods for incorporating concern about the sustainability of our ecological life-support system, nor do they adequately account for the value of ecological systems in contributing to our well-being.

Nature by the Numbers

One of the more important manifestations of this problem is that it creates major misperceptions about how well the economy is doing. Gross National Product (the total "value" of all the nation's goods and services in a given year), as well as other related measures of national economic performance have come to be extremely important as policy objectives, political issues and benchmarks of the general welfare. Yet GNP as presently defined ignores the contribution of nature to production, often leading to peculiar results.

For example, a standing forest provides real economic services for people: by conserving soil, cleaning air and water, providing habitat for wildlife, and supporting recreational activities. But as GNP is currently figured, only the value of harvested timber is calculated in the total. On the other hand, the billions of dollars that Exxon spent on the *Valdez* cleanup—and the billions spent by Exxon and others on the more than 100 other oil spills in the last 16 months—all actually *improved* our apparent economic performance. Why? Because cleaning up oil spills creates jobs and consumes resources, all of which add to GNP. Of course, these expenses would not have been necessary if the oil had not been spilled, so they shouldn't be considered "benefits." But GNP adds up all production without differentiating between costs and benefits, and is therefore not a very good measure of economic health.

In fact, when resource depletion and degradation are factored into economic trends, what emerges is a radically different picture from that depicted by conventional methods. Herman Daly and John

51

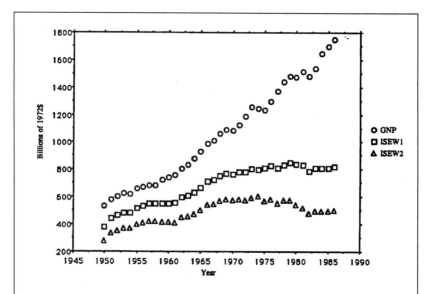

Figure 1: Herman Daly of the World Bank and John J. Cobb of the Claremont School of Theology calculated an "Index of Sustainable Economic Welfare" (ISEW) that adjusts GNP to account for pollution effects, environmental services and other ecological factors. A second version (ISEW2) also includes adjustments for depletion of non-renewable resources and long-term environmental damage. By this adjusted measure, Americans are much less "wealthy" than they seem. Source: Daly and Cobb, "For the Common Good: Redirecting the Economy Toward Community, the Environment, and a Sustainable Future"; Beacon Press, Boston.

Cobb have attempted to adjust GNP to account mainly for depletions of natural capital, pollution effects, and income distribution effects by producing an "index of sustainable economic welfare" (ISEW). The illustration above shows two versions of their index compared to GNP over the period from 1950 to 1986. What is strikingly clear is that while GNP rose over this interval, ISEW remained relatively unchanged since about 1970. When factors such as loss of farms and wetlands, costs of mitigating acid rain effects, and health costs caused by increased pollution are accounted for, the economy has not improved at all. If we continue to ignore natural ecosystems we may drive the economy down while we think we are building it up. By consuming our natural capital, we endanger our ability to sustain income.

A Sustainable Economy

"Sustainability" does not necessarily mean a stagnant economy, but we must be careful to distinguish between "growth" and "development." Economic growth, which is an increase in quantity, cannot be sustainable indefinitely on a finite planet. Economic development, which is an improvement in the quality of life without necessarily causing an increase in quantity of resources consumed, may be sustainable. Sustainable growth is an impossibility. Sustainable development must become our primary long-term policy goal.

Sustainability has been variously construed; but a useful definition is the amount of consumption that can be sustained indefinitely without degrading capital stocks—including "natural capital" stocks. In a business, capital stock includes long-term assets such as buildings and machinery that serve as the means of production. Natural capital is the soil and atmospheric structure, plant and animal biomass, etc. that, taken together, forms the basis of all ecosystems. This natural capital stock uses primary inputs (sunlight) to produce the range of ecosystem services.

To achieve sustainability, we must incorporate ecosystem goods and services into our economic accounting. The first step is to determine values for them comparable to those of economic goods and services. For example: We know what it costs to build and run sewage treatment plants. Since natural ecosystems perform these same services for free, they are worth at least the amount we would pay for corresponding human-produced services.

In determining values we must also consider how much of our ecological life support systems we can afford to lose. To what extent can we substitute manufactured for natural capital, and how much of our natural capital is irreplaceable? For example, could we replace the radiation screening services of the ozone layer if it were destroyed?

Some argue that we cannot place economic value on such "intangibles" as human life, environmental aesthetics, or long-term ecological benefits. But, in fact, we do so every day. When we set construction standards for highways, bridges and the like, we value human life—acknowledged or not—because spending more money on construction would save lives. To preserve our natural capital, we must confront these often difficult choices and valuations directly rather than denying their existence.

Because of the inherent difficulties and uncertainties in determining values, ecological economics acknowledges several different independent approaches. The conventional economic view defines value as the expression of human preferences, with the preferences taken as given and with no attempt to analyze their origins or patterns of long-term change. For goods and services with few long-term impacts (like tomatoes or bread) that are traded in well-functioning markets with adequate information, market ("revealed preference") valuations work well.

But ecological goods and services (like wetland sewage treatment or global climate control) are long-term by nature, are generally not traded in markets (no one owns the air or water), and information about their contribution to individual well-being is poor. To determine their value, economists try to get people to reveal what they would be willing to pay for ecological goods and services in hypothetical markets. For example, we can ask people the maximum they would pay to use national parks, even if they don't have to actually pay it. The quality of results in this method depends on how well informed people are; and it does not adequately incorporate long-term goals since it excludes future generations from bidding in the markets.

An alternative method for determining ecological values assumes a biophysical basis for value. This theory suggests that in the long run humans come to value things according to how costly they are to produce, and that this cost is ultimately a function of how organized they are relative to their environment. To organize a complex structure takes energy, both directly in the form of fuel and indirectly in the form of other organized structures like factories. For example a car is a much more organized structure than a lump of iron ore, and therefore it takes a lot of energy (direct and indirect) to organize iron ore into a car. The amount of solar energy required to grow forests can therefore serve as a measure of their energy cost, their organization, and hence their value.

The point that must be stressed is that the economic value of ecosystems is connected to their physical, chemical, and biological role in the long-term, global system—whether the present generation fully recognizes that role or not. If it is accepted that each species, no matter how seemingly uninteresting or lacking in immediate utility, has a role in natural ecosystems (which do provide many direct benefits to humans), it is possible to shift the focus away from our imperfect short-term perceptions and derive more accurate values for long-term ecosystem services. We may be able to estimate the values contributed by, say, maintenance of water and atmospheric quality to long-term human well-being. [See box]

Putting a Price on Swampland

How can we calculate the value of ecosystems? One of us (Costanza) and Steve Farber of Louisiana State University recently completed a study of the value of coastal wetlands in Louisiana (Table 1). We used two different valuation techniques: willingness-to-pay (WTP) and energy analysis (EA).

WTP valuation estimates individual's willingness-to-pay for the benefits of wetlands—in this case, for four major categories: commercial fishing, trapping, recreation, and storm protection. We did not include two other categories of willingness-to-pay: to preserve wetlands because they may one day visit them (option value) or simply to know that wetlands exist (existence value) even though we recognize that they are significant.

To estimate recreation values, for example, two techniques were used. The first simply asked recreational users what they would be willing to pay to use the wetlands. The problem with this technique is that respondents may answer "strategically." For example, if they think they may actually have to pay what they say, they may give a value lower than their true value. On the other hand, if they think their response may increase the probability of implementing a project they desire, they may state a value higher than their true value. The second technique (which was the primary means used) estimates WTP from what it actually costs users to travel there, such as plane fare, boat rental, gas and mileage costs and so forth.

The EA technique uses the solar energy captured by ecosystems as a measure of their value. To estimate this energy in wetlands

---

Table 1. Summary of Wetland Value Estimates (1983 dollars). From Costanza, R., S. C. Farber, and J. Maxwell. 1989. Valuation and management of wetland ecosystems. *Ecological Economics.* 1:335–362

Method	Per Acre Present Value at specified discount rate	
	8%	3%
Willingness To Pay based		
Commercial Fishery	$ 317	$ 846
Trapping	151	401
Recreation	46	181
Storm Protection	1915	7549
Total	$2429	$8977
Option and Existence Values	?	?
Energy Analysis based		
GPP conversion	6,400-10,600	17,000-28,200
"Best Estimate"	$2429-6400	$8977-17,000

we measured the Gross Primary Production (GPP) or the amount of solar energy captured and stored in plants. GPP is the basis for the food chain which supports the production of economically valuable products such as fish and wildlife. By converting GPP to a value based on what it would cost to produce the same energy with fossil fuels we can put a dollar value on this energy. This technique does not require a detailed listing of all the specific benefits of wetlands, but it may overestimate their value if some of the wetland products and services are not useful (directly or indirectly) to society.

Depending on the method of valuation and the discount rate assumed (the discount rate converts future annual values into their equivalent value in the present), our "best estimate" of the economic value of Louisiana coastal wetlands lies between $2,500 and $17,000 for every acre of marsh. The market value, exclusive of mineral rights, is about $500 an acre.

Toward Ecological Economics

Current systems of regulation are not very efficient at managing environmental resources for sustainability, particularly in the face of uncertainty about long-term values and impacts. They are inherently reactive rather than proactive. They induce legal confrontation, obfuscation, and government intrusion into business. Rather than encouraging long-range technical and social innovation, they tend to suppress it. They do not mesh well with the market signals that firms and individuals use to make decisions and do not effectively translate long-term global goals into short-term local incentives.

We need to explore promising alternatives to our current command and control environmental management systems, and to modify existing government agencies and other institutions accordingly. The enormous uncertainty about local and transnational environmental impacts needs to be incorporated into decision-making. We also need to better understand the sociological, cultural, and political criteria for acceptance or rejection of policy instruments.

One example of an innovative policy instrument currently being studied is a flexible environmental assurance bonding system designed to incorporate environmental criteria and uncertainty into the market system, and to induce positive environmental technological innovation.

In addition to direct charges for known environmental damages, a company would be required to post an assurance bond equal to the current best estimate of the largest potential future environmental damages; the money would be kept in interest-bearing escrow accounts. The bond (plus a portion of the interest) would be returned if the firm could show that the suspected damages had not occurred or would not occur. If they did, the bond would be used to rehabilitate or repair the environment and to compensate injured parties. Thus, the burden of proof would be shifted from the public to the resource-user and a strong economic incentive would be provided to research the true costs of environmentally innovative activities and to develop cost-effective pollution control technologies. This is an extension of the "polluter pays" principle to "the polluter pays for uncertainty as well."

Ecological economic thinking leads us to conclude that instead of being mesmerized into inaction by scientific uncertainty over our future, we should acknowledge uncertainty as a fundamental part of the system. We must develop better methods to model and value ecological goods and services, and devise policies to translate those values into appropriate incentives. If we continue to segregate ecology and economics we are courting disaster.

Energy — Doing More with Less

Chapter 5

ENVIRONMENTALLY ADVANCED TECHNOLOGY

by Robert L. Olson

As the Cold War ends and the danger of a large-scale nuclear war recedes, another challenge, nearly as critical for our destiny, demands attention: learning how to work out a sustainable, long-term fit between our growing technological civilization and the earth's ecological systems.

The truth is that no one really knows yet, in any detail, how to work out that long-term fit. All our government and corporate leaders are acting today without having in mind any realistic picture of "a future that works" both economically and ecologically.

A future in which 8 to 12 billion people attempt to adopt U.S. technology and lifestyle patterns looks ecologically disastrous. A future where today's high-consumption societies keep growing but the four-fifths of the world's people who live at low consumption levels stay that way (i.e., poor) looks socially as well as ecologically disastrous. The widening disparity in wealth would eventually lead to angry terrorism and "wars of redistribution," and poverty itself is a cause of many of the worst ecological problems in the Third World. A "no growth" future looks equally disastrous. The World Commission on Environment and Development estimated that at least a fivefold increase in world economic activity will be needed over the next 50 years just to meet the basic needs of a burgeoning world population and to begin reducing mass poverty.

"A future that works" will have to be a future where we succeed in sharply reducing our environmental impacts even though we are in the midst of a dynamic process of cooperative global development. We have hardly begun to appreciate the magnitude of this challenge and how greatly it will shape our outlooks and priorities over the next several generations.

Whole Pattern Shift

The changes that will probably be necessary for meeting this challenge, here and in the other industrial nations, add up to a "whole pattern shift" in our thinking and behavior. If we succeed, we will do it by moving away from extremes of conspicuous consumption and a "throwaway society." Economic theory and policy will be reshaped in the light of our growing understanding of the web of interconnections uniting the economy with the global ecosystem of which it is a part. Narrow goals like "U.S. competitiveness" will be incorporated into broader goals like "sustainable growth."

Governance at all levels, local to global, will take greater responsibility for our enormous power in nature. National governments, acting on a broad social consensus around environmental values, will make their departments of agriculture, defense, energy, state, and trade directly responsible for fostering environmental sustainability. Local and regional development will be increasingly shaped by concepts such as "bioregions" and "ecologically healthy cities." A more advanced technology, both more productive and more in harmony with nature, will prove absolutely necessary if the industrial world is to maintain anything like its present standard of living and the developing countries are to raise theirs to a similar level.

Other less tangible changes may be the most important of all. To succeed, we will need to adopt a more holistic perspective that pays attention to the interconnections of things, the side effects of actions, the long-term big picture of "what it is all about." Environmental politics will shed some of its adversarial "us vs. them" character as responsible groups representing different constituencies reach greater consensus on long-term goals and work together to assimilate new evidence, new theories, and surprise events. We will increasingly conceive of ourselves—experience ourselves—as members of a single human family, a single species that is a manifestation of nature, not above or outside of nature. Our conception of progress will shift from a rather one-sided preoccupation with technology and material growth to a balancing concern for ecological stewardship and "human development" in all its many dimensions. We will keep alive in our children a love of nature, and instill in them a sense of responsibility for protecting and restoring the natural world.

Taken together, these changes constitute what Alvin Toffler calls a "change of civilization." They range far beyond the level of reform that can be implemented by passing legislation or creating a new agency. Yet every one of these changes is being talked about today, and many of them are beginning to occur. Among environmentalists, most of these changes are becoming the new "conventional wisdom."

There is one change, however, that environmentalists themselves tend to resist: the idea that we need a more advanced technology. This is a serious situation, because only a more advanced technology can reconcile our environmental and economic goals. It is important, therefore, to examine the conflict between opponents and proponents of advanced technology, and to explore what an environmentally advanced technology might be like.

Reconsidering Advanced Technology

The skepticism and uneasiness that many people who are most concerned about the environment feel toward advanced technology is easy to understand. After all, advanced technology has often seemed more like the key environmental problem than a key for solving the problems.

During the 1970s, environmental debates often seemed to polarize between advocates of large-scale, complex "high" technologies and advocates of more environmentally benign, small-scale, relatively "low" technologies. The "soft energy path" based on conservation and simple renewable energy technologies was pitted against the "hard path" based largely on nuclear fission. Organic farming challenged the intensive use of energy, fertilizers, pesticides, and herbicides in conventional industrial agriculture. And so on.

There seemed no room for compromise between these polarized positions. For the optimistic proponents of advanced technology, the main danger was that retreatist, anti-technology "prophets of doom" would be too influential, causing a collective loss of nerve.

Then we would tragically fail to reach the affluent, worldwide Superindustrial Society that lay only a few generations ahead. For the critics of advanced technology, the danger was that uncritical technological optimism could lead us to neglect that worsens global environmental problems, could overshoot limits to growth, and cause us to miss our only opportunity to create a human-scale society in balance with nature.

As important as those debates were at the time, I think something went wrong in them that has unnecessarily turned some environmentalists away from advanced technology and confused the situation ever since. Environmentalists as well as technological optimists sometimes accepted one or more of three serious misconceptions.

Misconception #1: A Truly Advanced Technology Already Exists

Both the champions and the critics of advanced technology have tended to define it in terms of existing technologies. But "high technology" is a moving target. The term was originally coined to describe the first great surge of science-based innovation in the 1880s that produced steel-frame construction, aluminum, the incandescent light bulb, rayon, the telephone, the electric locomotive, and the internal combustion engine. By the end of World War II, high technology meant developments like atomic energy, the first lumbering electronic computers, feedback control, and rocketry.

Now we are at the beginning—not the end—of the Information Revolution, the Biotechnology Revolution, Revolutions in Materials and Manufacturing, and an Energy Transition. Revolutionary changes are being conceived in areas like "Living Machines" and "Industrial Ecology." Later in the 21st century, our growing ability to manipulate matter at the molecular level could put our technology on an entirely new foundation and make all the curves of technological change head straight up. Within 50 years, nearly everything that passes for High Tech today is likely to be a museum piece.

So a little modesty seems in order about just how advanced today's technology really is. Science-based technology is not much more than a century old and still in its infancy. We need to think about advanced technology in terms of the possibilities ahead as well as our limited accomplishments to date.

Misconception #2: Advanced Technology is Always Big, Complex, and Environmentally Destructive

Critics of modern technology point with good cause to problems of scale and complexity, pollution, and health hazards. Some then go on to treat these problems as *inevitable characteristics* of advanced technology. But if we approach technology in terms of emerging potentials rather than present limitations, it makes more sense to view these problems as signs that we have not yet achieved a sufficiently advanced technology.

The recent flap over "cold fusion" is probably the most dramatic example of how a more advanced technology might actually be small, simple, safe, and nonpolluting. Conventional fusion research has focused on enormously expensive and complicated laser fusion devices and gigantic tokamaks for confining plasmas several times the temperature of the sun's interior. But in the spring of 1989, two scientists, Stanley Pons and Martin Fleischmann, announced that they were producing fusion energy with simple, tabletop devices at room temperature, and scientists around the world dropped everything and rushed to their labs. The jury is still out on cold fusion, and it may well turn out to be a bust, but the excitement it generated illustrates the values scientists share with most of the rest of us. Other things being equal, clean (fusion) is much better than dirty (fission); the "elegant simplicity" made possible by deep understanding is preferable to excessively complicated means or brute force; and miniaturization rather than bigness is often a hallmark of technological progress.

Solar photovoltaic (PV) technology provides another example of a small, simple, safe and nonpolluting advanced technology. In the energy debates of the 1970s, "hard path" proponents dismissed PV technology as too expensive to play a significant role, and "soft path" advocates often dismissed it as too high-tech and exotic. But now most business leaders and researchers in the field expect PV electricity to be cost-competitive with all other generating options by the turn of the century or shortly thereafter. Small-scale installations on rooftops will be as economical as utility-scale arrays. PV technology represents the ultimate in "elegant simplicity," with no moving parts and nothing to go wrong. And PV technologies emit no pollutants at all during their operation (the environmental challenge is to clean up the manufacturing process).

"High" technologies like solar cells often work best in combination with simpler, "soft technology" components. For example, even the most technically advanced energy-efficient home, using high-tech devices like solar cells, "occupancy sensors" and "smart lighting," must also include simple, cost-effective measures such as plugging leaks, insulating, and taking advantage of opportunities for passive solar heating.

Misconception #3: There is Only One Kind of Advanced Technology and it "Just Happens"

During the 1970s and 1980s, the image of the future offered by most technological optimists was essentially a bigger-better-faster-higher version of the present. The idea that advanced technology might evolve along sharply different alternative paths, defined by different value systems, was not an idea most technologists considered very seriously. The common view was that advanced technology is just advanced technology, and that its main characteristics just unfold as they unfold, even though you can get a competitive advantage by playing around with the details. Too often, in retrospect, environmentalists accepted this idea of a single type of advanced technology, didn't like it, and so defined themselves as techno-critics.

The idea of a single track of advanced technology that "just happens" seems plausible mainly because the unpredictable emergence of scientific knowledge "whose time has come" often does set the direction of technological change. But science is not, and never has been, a fully autonomous process with a direction set only by its internal logic. Research in thermodynamics was made possible by people who had both practical concerns (improved steam engines, gun boring) and funds to invest. The discovery of petroleum and the rapid growth of the oil industry steered chemistry away from research on wood and coal. Money available for research into tropical diseases has depended almost entirely on U.S. military involvement in malarial zones (during World War II and in Vietnam). The land grant college system stimulated research and education in agriculture. Most contraceptive development continues to be geared to middle-class markets in rich countries rather than to the needs of poor countries. Research in aerospace, microelectronics, lasers, and dozens of other fields is sustained by direct or indirect military support. So we need to be wary of creating a mythology of autonomy that obscures the extent to which science and science-based technology are steered by social choices.

We can choose to create an environmentally advanced technology.

A technology shaped by environmental values and drawing on the full potential of modern science will eventually be very different from a technology guided only by value-empty economics—but it will still be an advanced technology. This is a major change of perspective for some environmentalists, but it is one that is occurring. Gus Speth, President of World Resources Institute, puts it this way:

> "We must ditch 20th-century technologies and rapidly adopt those of the 21st century. Our old environmental foe, modern technology, must become a friend....
> ...only technology can save us. That is a hard thing for a congenital Luddite like myself to say, but, in a small victory of nurture over nature, I do now believe it. I do not diminish the importance of lifestyle changes—some go hand-in-hand with technological change—and I applaud the spread of more voluntary simplicity in our wasteful society. But economic growth has its imperatives; it will occur. The key question is: with what technologies? Only the population explosion rivals this question in fundamental importance to the planetary environment."

Nature As A Model

Nature itself provides a successful model of an environmentally advanced technology. The biosphere as it now exists is an enormously sophisticated system for gathering and using energy, recycling materials, and regulating the temperature, oxidation state, and many other variables to maintain conditions favorable for life.

Nature was not always so sophisticated. It took billions of years and many "inventions" in the course of biological evolution for the biosphere to reach its present level of "advanced biotechnics." In its earlier stages, nature often resembled our present, unsustainable industrial system. The earliest, fermentation-based forms of life lived by feeding on and using up a finite stock of organic molecules accumulated in the oceans during prebiotic time, just as today's unsustainable form of technological civilization is using up a finite stock of fossil fuels.

Nature solved its original "energy crisis" through one of the greatest innovations in the whole history of life—photosynthesis. Tapping into the abundant and inexhaustible energy of sunlight, prokaryotic photobacteria, the first photosynthesizers, produced glucose from atmospheric carbon dioxide, replacing the depleted store of organic molecules in the early oceans.

But the invention of photosynthesis had side effects that led to the Earth's first "environmental crisis." Photosynthesis produced oxygen as a waste product, and oxygen was highly toxic to fermentation-based organisms. Nature used a temporary "technological fix," organisms called stromatolites, to combine this free oxygen with iron dissolved in the oceans, creating the iron-rich hematite deposits which we mine as iron ores today. This quick fix only worked for a billion years or so. Then, as the dissolved iron in the oceans was used up, the oxygen level in the atmosphere began to rise sharply. The early biosphere faced a critical situation similar to the one we face today: it could neither tolerate nor recycle its own toxic wastes.

Nature responded with a surge of biotechnic innovation. A new type of oxygen-tolerant photobacteria emerged, the blue-green algae. Then another great innovation, respiration, allowed organisms to actually use oxygen "waste" in obtaining energy from organic molecules. The aerobic respirators required much less organic material to sustain them than the earlier anaerobic fermenters, and their yield of energy available for further metabolic processes was 18 times as high. The fermenters could not compete with the new energy- and resource-efficient respirators except in oxygen-free environments like sediments and deep oceans.

As oxygen-using photosynthesizers bloomed abundantly over the oceans and land masses, a second planetary environmental crisis probably occurred, a mirror image of today's "greenhouse effect." By burning fossil fuels, we are increasing the amount of carbon dioxide in the atmosphere, which will eventually cause the earth to heat up. The early photosynthesizers used the carbon dioxide in the air and oceans as food, and were rapidly eating the blanket that kept the Earth warm. The planet was saved from freezing because organisms called methanogens proliferated, returning the greenhouse gas, methane, and some carbon dioxide, to the air. British scientist James Lovelock argues that by this point life on earth had evolved into a sustainable, adaptive, self-regulating system that he calls Gaia, the name the ancient Greeks gave to their Goddess of the Earth.

Gaia soon manifested more and more sophisticated biotechnologies designed both to promote the development of life and to protect itself from environmental dangers. For example, marine life synthesized chemical compounds able to recycle nutritious elements abundant in the ocean and transfer them through the air to the land, making the land more hospitable for life. To protect life against salt concentrations in the ocean rising to a toxic level (about 6 percent by weight) probably required the building of vast limestone reefs to trap salt in evaporite lagoons. This planetary-scale "macroengineering" project dwarfs any construction project ever undertaken by human beings.

Even in its earliest stages, when the Earth was only populated by bacteria, the biosphere was a busy information-processing system. All life was linked by a slow but accurate genetic communications network, exchanging messages on low-molecular-weight nucleic acids. As living organisms evolved sense organs and complex nervous systems, "intelligence" became a significant variable in evolution. It is information processing, the vast majority of it not of a "conscious" type, that has made the biosphere's self-regulation and evolution possible.

Characteristics Of
An Environmentally Advanced Technology

The model provided by nature suggests some of the characteristics of an environmentally advanced technology. Above all, it will be sustainable: capable of satisfying present needs without jeopardizing the prospects of future generations; capable of being used by all people for all time without exhausting resources or having unacceptable environmental consequences.

A second characteristic is that it will be based on a safe and inexhaustible supply of energy. Like life itself 3 billion years ago, we are working out more efficient ways to capture and use the abundant energy of sunlight. Fusion is another possible "eternal" source of energy, if it can be made sufficiently safe and inexpensive. Fission is making a contribution as a transitional technology, but the problems it poses of nuclear weapons proliferation, accident and sabotage risks, and waste disposal make it a poor technology upon which to base a civilization.

A third characteristic is high efficiency in the use of energy and other resources. Efficiency substitutes "know-how" for matter and energy. Just as respiration and other innovations in evolution improved the efficiency of early life forms, so technical improvements in our production processes, buildings, and transportation systems will allow us to produce "outputs" (goods and services) with a small fraction of the energy "inputs" needed today. We already know how to double the practical efficiency of industrial motors and jet aircraft, triple the efficiency of lights, automobiles, and most household appliances, and increase the efficiency of buildings by factors ranging from two to ten. When we incorporate the environmental costs of producing and using energy into energy prices, most of these efficiency improvements will be economically attractive compared to the cost of any new kind of energy supplies. Efficiency reduces energy and material costs, and it also reduces environmental problems "at the source." More efficient production processes will use and pollute less water, use less wood leaving more trees standing, use less energy reducing the acid rain and greenhouse warming problems, and so on.

A fourth characteristic is high efficiency in recycling and the use of by-products. The biosphere is nearly a perfect recycling system. Plants synthesize nutrients from sunlight, soil, and air. Herbivores eat plants and provide food for carnivores whose wastes and bodies feed further generations of plants. Vast cycles in the soils, oceans, and atmosphere recirculate nutrients. Nothing goes to waste. With an environmentally advanced technology, our homes, communities, and the entire "Industrial Ecosystem" would function in an analogous way. Beyond optimizing the consumption of energy and materials and minimizing wastes, we would always use the effluents of any one process as a raw material for another process. Materials would never be seriously depleted: as in natural ecosystems, the industrial ecosystem would simply keep changing circulating stocks of material from one form to another. Renewable resources would be carefully managed on a "sustained yield" basis so that they would never be depleted. Pollution would be viewed as a design flaw, a failure to take advantage of some potentially useful resource. An ideal industrial ecosystem may never be possible in practice, but we will have to move toward this general model to meet the challenge of growing pollution and wastes and decreasing supplies of high-grade raw materials.

A fifth characteristic of an environmentally advanced technology is that it will be increasingly intelligent. The biosphere evolved from low-level genetic information processing to human intelligence. Similarly, our tools, which have been unintelligent and uncommunicating, are evolving to a higher level of information-processing capability. With tiny integrated circuit chips, intelligence (or simulated intelligence) is being embedded in more and more of those tools. We are moving toward a future where everything from automobile fuel consumption to industrial process control will be optimized by artificial intelligence. "Smart materials" will change their characteristics in response to internal and external conditions, giving us, for example, windows that become more transparent or opaque and change their insulation value depending on the interior temperature. The machines we use will increasingly be "glass boxes" rather than "black boxes," capable of advising us about what they can do, how they work, and how to use them efficiently and safely. Over time, the biosphere will be increasingly "wired" with monitoring instrumentation and satellite remote sensing, so we will know much more about the environmental impacts of everything we do.

A last characteristic of an environmentally advanced technology is that it will be increasingly "alive." Ecologist John Todd describes the emergence of a new field of ecological engineering and a new category of technology, "Living Machines." Living machines composed of many types of organisms and advanced structural materials can be designed to perform many of the most vital functions in society, including food and fuel production, waste treatment and water purification, and climate control within buildings. Living machines emulate the design principles used by nature itself and display characteristics of living systems such as self-repair and self-design to adapt to changing environmental conditions.

Looking ahead, physicist Freeman Dyson argues that we will increasingly have a choice between two different technological approaches, which he calls "grey" and "green." Grey technology is the familiar realm of mechanical moving parts, motors, and electronic circuits. Green technology is a new and still exotic realm of ecological engineering combined, over time, with genetic engineering. Dyson believes that green technology will come to the fore rapidly, and will become dominant within about fifty years, although grey technology will never be abandoned.

Green technology can have extremely low environmental impacts. It can provide a wide range of environmental services, from breaking down toxic wastes to rapidly restoring degraded ecosystems. It can miniaturize the production of essential services, making possible, for example, much more intensive ways of growing food, so that more land can be left in a natural state. And working out the design principles of a green technology will help us understand the functioning of the forests, prairies, estuaries and other great ecological systems within which we live. The shift from "grey" toward "green" will be a major shift toward a more environmentally advanced technology.

The Opportunity Ahead

If the outlook I am presenting is even roughly valid, then virtually every technology we use will be redesigned and rebuilt during the 21st century. Whole new forms of technology will come into existence.

This transformation of technology will be both pushed and pulled by enormous social forces. It will be "pushed" by accelerating environmental deterioration—climatic change from the greenhouse effect, ozone depletion, the rapid destruction of forests, the spread of deserts, the loss of millions of species of plants and animals, soil erosion, water scarcity, toxic contamination, air and water pollution. In a situation of rapidly worsening environmental impacts on a global scale and a growing understanding that the success of human civilization is ultimately at stake, the social and political pressure for creating environmentally advanced technologies will become enormous.

An environmentally advanced technology will also be "pulled" into existence by positive images of what the future could be like. Unlike the 1970s, when some seemed to counsel a kind of "safety of the tombs"—a step back to a more static society with less advanced technologies—the 1990s is bringing a new image of a technology that is more advanced in every sense, including its ability to operate in harmony with nature.

The other great social force that will "pull" an environmentally advanced technology into existence is the unprecedented opportunity it offers for business. Creating an environmentally advanced technology will provide enormous business opportunities in the 1990s and over the next 50 years. Vast new industries related to the redesign of manufacturing processes, the re-use of waste materials, energy efficiency, renewable energy, efficient transportation, sustainable agriculture, and a completely new realm of green technology await development.

The challenge of building these new industries will change the social context of environmentalism. In our society, where the private sector controls nearly all of the resources for developing new knowledge into new products, an environmentally advanced technology can only be brought into existence through the full involvement of business. The adversarial environmental politics of the past, appropriate for challenging the destructive impacts of a previous technological order, will tend to shift toward negotiated, consensual efforts to foster investment in a new technological order in harmony with nature. Government will play a key role in supporting R&D and creating policy incentives that make it in the private sector's self-interest to move in this direction.

If we succeed, people in the future will look back at late 20th-century technology as primitive and totally unsustainable—based on depleting resources, inefficient and wasteful, and crashing around against people and ecological systems like the proverbial bull in a china shop. They will wonder how anyone could have seriously asserted that this was an "advanced technology."

Chapter 6

THE SUN
AS RENEWABLE RESOURCE
Fossil-Free Future
by Bill Keepin

Global warming, acid rain, air pollution, oil spills, nuclear waste, nuclear proliferation, deforestation, the debt crisis, and even much of the world's military tension are all partially or entirely attributable to a single source: the inefficient use of nonrenewable energy. The links are direct, and the scale of any one of these threats is sufficient to justify immediate corrective action. Taken together, these problems constitute a profound global crisis that calls for dramatic action to eliminate dependence on nuclear and fossil fuels.

Renewable energy technologies inherently ameliorate or eliminate every one of the aforementioned problems. However, energy planners worldwide hold the belief that renewable energy will never provide a significant share of future energy needs. This view is based on experience and data that are now way out of date. Renewable energy technologies have made dramatic progress over the past several years, and energy efficiency greatly reduces future requirements for energy. Thus the combined potential of renewable energy and energy efficiency is dramatic, as discussed below.

Renewable energy technologies perform better and cost less than ever before. Wind power has matured with a three-fold drop in cost over the past decade, and electricity generated from wind is now competitive for intermediate and peak power in the United States. The cost of electricity generated from biomass is roughly half what new coal-fired power costs. Perhaps the most promising developments are in solar energy technologies, which are reviewed in more detail below.

Solar Photovoltaic Technology

Solar photovoltaic (PV) technology converts sunlight directly into electricity—with no moving parts, no fuel, and no noise or smoke. Dramatic advances have been made in the past few years with thin-film amorphous-silicon technologies and other flat-plate collector designs. Silicon is much less hazardous than other PV materials, and a recent review concludes that large-scale implementation of PV systems based on silicon technologies will (at worst) cause no greater environmental problems than producing conventional energy systems. Operation of these systems will be harmless, since no pollutants are emitted. The potential for solar photovoltaic (PV) technology was recently assessed by the United States Department of Energy (DOE). The DOE is hardly a solar advocacy group—in fact its assessment has been widely criticized by renewable energy advocates for being too conservative and pessimistic. Yet the assessment is remarkable, and it overturns many widespread myths about PV technology.

Consider some of the DOE's findings: PV can be used effectively anywhere in the United States, including under the gray skies of the northeast. PV electricity production requires no more land than coal-fired electricity, and no water. PV sales are currently expanding at 30% per year, and the cost of PV is expected to drop from today's value of 20 to 40 cents per kWh to 4 cents per kWh by 2030, or possibly sooner. Rather than the usual incremental growth, there is a likelihood of explosive growth in the PV market when the price reaches about 8 cents per kWh, which could happen as early as the year 2000. Thus, according to the DOE assessment, "the ultimate role of PV may be far larger than most assume," and the conclusion is that "PV appears to be a long-term and desirable solution to U.S. and global concerns for energy and environment." See the Appendix following this chapter for more extended quotations from the DOE assessment.

Critics of the DOE assessment argue that its time estimates for implementation are too conservative, and that things could happen much more quickly, given the requisite R&D funding. A recent assessment of the potential for a solar hydrogen economy from Princeton University and the World Resources Institute suggests that cheap PV electricity could be available much sooner. Based on detailed examination of current laboratory and field experience, the Princeton study concludes that by the year 2000, DC electricity could be produced from solar PV in sunny regions for 2 to 3.5 cents per kilowatt-hour (c/kWh), and that baseload AC electricity with underground pumped hydro storage could be produced for 5 to 8 c/kWh. Taken together, the DOE and Princeton assessments of the potential for solar PV electricity seriously challenge conventional thinking about solar energy, and they suggest that clean solar electricity will be available for just a few cents per kWh sometime between 2000 and the year 2030.

Applications of solar PV technology are myriad. Currently the largest market is for remote power, but cells may also be placed on rooftops of existing residential homes and commercial buildings, or concentrated in large power plants. If a program were implemented to install PV systems in 10 percent of the 2 million new houses built each year, 4,000 MW of utility peaking power could be displaced by the year 2000. A utility-scale prototype photovoltaic power plant with capacity exceeding 3 MW is now being built in California. A PV-powered aircraft made its maiden flight across the United States in July 1990. The futuristic design utilizes solar cells made of amorphous silicon on a transparent plastic substrate, giving them the flexibility to adhere to the curved wing surface. The aircraft resembles a high-performance glider with a propeller, and is capable of speeds of up to 160 km per hour.

Solar Hydrogen

The Princeton study mentioned above also explores the possibility of a solar hydrogen future in the United States and the world. Hydrogen is probably the cleanest known energy carrier, and when it burns in air, the major combustion product is ordinary steam. It produces no carbon dioxide, carbon monoxide, sulfur oxides, ozone, particulates, or volatile organic compounds. The *Hindenburg* zeppelin disaster has left hydrogen psychologically branded as an unsafe fuel, but actual experience has shown that hydrogen is no more dangerous than gasoline or natural gas. The Princeton assessment examined the possibility of producing hydrogen electrolytically in sunny regions and piping it to less sunny regions. With minor modification, today's natural-gas pipeline system could be used for this purpose. Prices for delivered hydrogen could be between $1.70 and $2.35 per U.S. gallon gasoline equivalent by the year 2000. Land requirements would not be a serious limiting constraint, as is often assumed. To displace all fossil fuels with PV hydrogen in the United States would require an area of land roughly equal to that of the U.S. highway system (about 1 percent of the land area), much of which would be on rooftops. To displace all fossil fuels worldwide would require 1.7 percent of the world's deserts, equivalent in area to just 3.6 percent of the land currently committed to agriculture. Centralized hydrogen plants would be located in remote semi-arid regions, where there is little or no competition for land use. Water requirements would be remarkably low: less than one-fifth of the rainfall that falls naturally on the collector area (even in desert regions).

Critics will argue that the Princeton assessment is overly optimistic, and that even if the detailed technological and economic analyses are correct, institutional and sociopolitical inertia have not been taken into account. It is obvious that a shift to solar electricity and hydrogen would require major investments in capital and infrastructure, with associated institutional structures—but this is no less true of other long-term energy strategies, such as a global buildup of nuclear power. Indeed, growing environmental concern with fossil fuels and mounting health and safety concerns with nuclear power and radioactive waste may act as a catalyst for rapid change in energy policy worldwide.

Solar Thermal Energy

Solar thermal technology entails the use of a parabolic-trough-shaped mirror that directs the sun's rays onto a pipe situated along the mirror's focal axis. Water or oil is heated in the pipe, which is insulated with a transparent insulator (consisting of an evacuated tube and a selective surface that minimizes heat loss). This produces steam directly, or both steam and electricity in solar cogeneration plants. The technology is currently employed to generate electricity in large-scale plants in the deserts of California and Israel. Installed capacity in California is nearly 200 MW today, and another 600 to 1000 MW are projected to be built. Today's plants have natural gas-fired backup to ensure uninterrupted power during peak demand periods. Costs of electricity generation have dropped from 24 cents per kWh in 1984 to under 8 cents per kWh in 1989, and are expected to drop further to 5 cents per kWh for plants coming on line in 1994. Thus the technology has rapidly evolved to a clean, economically competitive source of electricity.

Perhaps the greatest potential for solar thermal technology in the future lies not in the utility-scale applications, but rather in smaller-scale on-site applications of the technology. Residential and commercial solar thermal systems could produce low-temperature heat for space heating, cooking, water heating, etc. Small solar thermal systems can produce steam directly, or both steam and electricity. Low-temperature steam is the preferred (or required) heat source for many industrial processes, and solar thermal technology is well suited to produce low- to medium-temperature steam (160 to 200 degrees Centigrade). Research is currently underway to explore the possibility of producing high-temperature steam (500 to 600 degrees Centigrade). Recent solar thermal systems are designed to have low capital and maintenance costs. This is achieved using elegant designs that minimize expensive components and eliminate most moving parts. For example, the omission of tracking systems (to follow the sun's daily motion) offers a tremendous improvement in simplicity, reliability, and cost—while incurring only a 10 percent penalty in energy output.

One of the world's most profound and least-recognized energy crises is the shortage of cooking fuel in poor nations. Solar thermal technologies show remarkable promise for application in the Third World. Mindful of numerous past failures with renewable-technology transfer in developing countries, today's solar thermal designs are extremely robust and simple, requiring little or no maintenance. For example, a solar thermal stove has been developed that can be used any time of day or night. Water is heated in two solar thermal collectors (each measuring about 2 by 8 feet) and stored at modest pressure in an insulated storage tank. The collectors are installed on the roof, drawing water up automatically from the tank (thermosyphon effect), and the accumulated energy is stored in the form of superheated water (180 to 200 degrees Centigrade and seven atmospheres of pressure, equivalent to the pressure of a normal butane or oxygen tank). The entire system is closed except for an over-pressure release valve, and there are no pumps, gauges, or moving parts. The water never comes into contact with the air; it serves only as a medium for heat transfer, for which it is well suited. Maintenance consists of moving a lever one notch each month to keep the collectors pointed toward the average position of the sun in the sky, and occasional cleaning (the mirror surface is self-cleaning in the rain). The only breakable part is the evacuated glass tube with selective surface, which slips easily on and off the focal axis for ease of replacement. The storage tank is approximately spherical in shape, about 16 inches in diameter, with a flat top that serves as the hot plate. The tank is enclosed in 4 inches of insulation, with a lid to gain access to the hot plate. The stove works any time of day or night, and performs much like an electric hot plate. It will boil a pan of water in a few minutes.

Nuclear versus Solar

Advocates of nuclear power argue that it may be the answer for tomorrow's clean energy, because it produces negligible airborne pollution. However, not only are the health and safety problems with nuclear power and radioactive waste continuing to mount, but progress in solar technologies has been so striking that solar energy can now produce comparable quantities of energy, just as efficiently. The Princeton study mentioned above draws the following comparison between solar PV technology and nuclear power. The allure of nuclear power is that small quantities of fuel can produce large quantities of energy. Cycled through fast breeder reactors (the most efficient nuclear technology), a single gram of uranium can produce 3,800 kWh of electricity. However, a uranium atom can only be fissioned once, whereas a silicon solar cell can absorb photons repeatedly and convert them to electricity. Over its lifetime in 15%-efficient thin-film PV solar cells, one gram of silicon produces 3,300 kWh of electricity. Thus, gram for gram, silicon and uranium produce comparable amounts of electricity, and silicon is 5000 times more abundant in the earth's crust. Silicon accounts for half the mass of ordinary sand, and the electricity that could be produced from one ton of sand is equivalent to that from burning over half a million tons of coal.

Nuclear proponents are still hopeful about prospects for future passively safe reactor designs, smaller modular reactors, and of course the ultimate promise of thermonuclear fusion. But all of these efforts appear increasingly unnecessary, because today's solar energy technologies already achieve every dream of nuclear power research: its resource potential is unlimited, its energy source is fusion (with a self-containing "reactor" located a comfortable 93 million miles away), it is clean, it is passively safe, it has minimal waste and environmental problems, it comes in all sizes from rooftop to utility-scale, and its fuel is effectively infinite (sunlight and sand). The only thing left to do is to bring down the cost, which will not be difficult according to informed assessments. Thus the only nuclear research questions of genuine relevance for the future are how to deal with nuclear waste, how to decommission nuclear plants, and how to prevent further proliferation of nuclear weapons.

Conclusion

The myth that renewable energy technologies will never produce much energy is still very widespread. This chapter has explored recent developments, which point to quite the opposite conclusion. Breakthroughs in renewable energy technologies are happening so fast that it is difficult to keep pace with them. The recent DOE and Princeton assessments are part of a growing body of evidence that overturns conventional thinking about renewable energy. Both assessments portend auspicious prospects for solar energy that were unthinkable even a few years ago. Both project that the cost of pollution-free electricity produced from the sun will drop to a few pennies per kilowatt-hour (with storage). In the meantime, wind power and biomass technologies already achieve this target, and they are generating electricity for less than the cost of new coal-fired or nuclear power.

When combined with energy efficiency, the potential of renewable energy is remarkable indeed. The DOE's own studies show that the potential for renewable energy in the United States by the year 2010 is 80 to 90 quads, more than all the energy consumed in the United States today. One consequence is that nuclear power appears increasingly irrelevant to a sustainable global energy future. It simply will not be needed—either as fission or fusion. Renewable sources already produce more energy than nuclear power in the United States, which has the largest nuclear program in the world. It is estimated that by 2010, up to 80 percent of the nation's energy could be supplied from renewable energy sources, and this takes no account of the potential for a hydrogen economy as discussed above. Of course much work remains to be done and new challenges will be encountered, but the vision of a clean, sustainable, all-renewable energy future is taking shape on the horizon.

Appendix
U.S. Department of Energy Review of Photovoltaic Electricity

The following text is selected from an assessment prepared by five U.S. national laboratories for the United States Department of Energy: The Potential of Renewable Energy: An Interlaboratory White Paper, Washington, DC: SERI/TP-260-3674, DE 90000322, United States Department of Energy, March 1990, pp G1 through G11.

Photovoltaics is one of the most benign forms of electricity generation likely to be available in the next 50 years. It requires low operation and maintenance (O&M) expenditures, no fuel, no fumes, no noise, and no cooling water, greatly increasing its value in the United States and the world. . . . The efficiency of today's flat plate modules ranges from about 5% to almost 15%. . . . The largest use of PV today is the remote-power market. . . . The current rapid growth rate in PV sales (more than 30% annually) is almost exclusively because of the increase in sales for remote power. . . . The current utility purchases for PV are relatively small, but very important. The potential of PV to displace very significant amounts of conventional energy is based in large part on the fact that the main resource of PV—sunlight—is almost ubiquitous. About 700 times the total annual energy used by the United States falls on this country as sunlight. Clearly, the resource is immense. Just as significantly, PV systems are not geographically limited by sunlight variations in the United States. All PV systems, except those based on concentrators, can be used everywhere in the United States, including the upper Midwest and the Northeast. This is because PV systems produce a fixed proportion of the annual sunlight as electricity, and annual sunlight varies by 25% from an average U.S. value of about 1800 kWh/m2 (the amount available in Kansas City for a module not tracking the sun)....

Today's record PV efficiencies for laboratory cells can be expected to appear as commercial module efficiencies before the turn of the century. In fact, today's laboratory cell efficiencies are already high enough (10% to 30%) to permit significant market penetration if they were module efficiencies.... Of course, progress depends on ongoing funding both by industry and DOE. The PV industry is still young and hence very fragile. But PV costs are dropping rapidly and some markets are taking off; the outlook today is much better than it was even 2 years ago.... [A] major opportunity to reduce costs is to develop the manufacturing and processing capabilities needed to produce PV on a large scale.... One serious constraint for the U.S. industry could be the commitment of foreign-owned industry ... Germany's PV budget alone is 65% larger than the U.S. budget; Japan's is 40% greater....

Except in the U.S. West, land is perceived as a constraint for the development of PV by utilities, but forward-thinking utilities are already testing PV either on customers' rooftops or on their own land.... The space needs are equivalent for dispersed or central station generation systems. A recent study by DOE shows that PV land requirements (on a per kilowatt-hour basis) are very similar to those for coal production and combustion.... PV systems can be put on rooftops or can use land without competing uses (ie, deserts and land with no water access).... Materials availability is also not a constraint because the amounts of semiconductor material used in the PV cell are small or because the materials are as common in nature as sand. PV's small requirements for semiconductor material can be best understood via a comparison with nuclear power. For a breeder reactor with 50% fuel recycling, 1 g of uranium produces about 4 MWh of electricity. For a thin-film module (layers of 0.3 to 1.0 x 10-6 m thickness), there are about 2 g of semiconductor for each square meter of module area. Over a 30-year life, a 10%-efficient module (1 m2 in size) would produce about 6 MWh of electricity in a typical U.S. location (e.g., Kansas City). Thus, the PV output (about 3 MWh/g) and the output of a breeder reactor (with fuel recycling) would be about the same. . . . In summary, PV appears to be a long-term and desirable solution to U.S. and global concerns for energy and environment. Other countries clearly recognize the opportunity. . . .

The kinds of costs that we ultimately expect PV to reach—as low as 4 c/kWh (without premium)—suggest that PV with storage to meet almost any electrical load will be affordable. . . . PV has advantages in terms of fuel production [e.g., hydrogen]: (1) it is efficient enough to minimize the need for large tracts of land, and (2) it uses so little water that it can be located on land with few competing uses (e.g., the desert). But because these important possibilities remain speculative, we have not included any PV market contribution from them. However, our cost projection of 4 c/kWh in 2030 . . . suggests that the ultimate role of PV may be far larger than most assume. Two representatives of the U.S. PV industry who reviewed this white paper believe that the levelized cost of PV will drop substantially faster than projected here. In addition, input we received from other reviewers suggested the same thing, i.e., that our expectations about future reductions in PV prices are too pessimistic. . . . Reviewers also criticized our market projections as too pessimistic. One introduced the concept of a period of explosive growth. We had assumed steady, incremental growth. . . . About 8 c/kWh was proposed as the price level at which growth would become explosive. After this period (about 10 years), growth would follow more normal trends. Given the modular quality of PV manufacture and the fact that it is amenable to automation, we agree with the reviewer about the possibility of explosive growth in the PV industry. . . . A period of explosive growth could occur about 2020 [or 2010 or 2005 depending on the DOE scenario considered]. In fact, if progress is more rapid, around 2000. . . . PV is a new, untried technology. Its future is uncertain. We can project the success of PV based on the physics of PV devices. We know they will work, and we foresee that they will become inexpensive. However, at this point our tools for projecting cost trends and market penetrations 30 to 40 years into the future are too weak. The reader can use the various projections here as an envelope of possibilities.

Chapter 7

ENERGY EFFICIENCY— NOT DENIAL
Economic and Environmental Profit

by Ted Flanigan

Energy efficiency, unlike so many personal and policy decisions, affords a win-win solution: providing positive economic and environmental profit. The potentials for energy efficiency in our society and around the globe are simply huge. Using currently available technologies coupled with innovative regulation and financing, we can reduce overall energy consumption by 75%. This can profit our society enormously, saving nearly $300 billion per year and improving our standard of living.

While reducing energy consumption through behavioral change is meritorious (carpooling, setting back thermostats, turning out the lights, etc.), it is not the subject of this chapter. Energy conservation carries a lot of "baggage:" expectations of being colder in the winter, hotter in the summer—worse yet—warm beer and short showers! The term conservation obscures recent technological developments. We simply do not need to use so much energy to provide the services that we desire. Far from deprivation, energy efficiency provides equal or better services. Use of the term energy productivity may be even more palatable: simply wringing more work out of each unit of energy.

The challenge of tapping the gross technical potential for energy efficiency is large. Fortunately, just as awesome as the institutional barriers is the progress that has been made with technologies for energy efficiency, and innovation in regulatory reform and financing. Furthermore, a multitude of successful demonstration energy efficiency programs are validating the early claims of analysts: efficiency can be "brought on line" quickly and inexpensively. So far from accepting energy growth as fate, we must recognize that we have control over the destiny of our energy intensity.

The U.S. has had some experience in energy efficiency. The national response to the two oil shocks in the 1970s deserves a mixed report card. Total energy consumption in the United States was flat from 1972-1985 while GNP grew by 40%, shattering the myth that in order for our society to prosper our energy consumption must grow in parallel with economic indicators. In 1973, per capita energy consumption was 285 million BTUs (British Thermal Units); in 1989 it was only 246 million BTUs. The national response was prompted by concerns of dependency on OPEC to fulfill a seemingly unending thirst for oil. But now our dependence on foreign oil has reached an all-time high, and only a smattering of efficiency improvements have been implemented in our society, as low oil prices have allowed for sloppy consumption patterns. And the impressive gains in efficiency that kept energy consumption flat only revealed the tip of the iceberg.

Now, concerns about energy use relate to environmental destruction and specifically acid rain and the threat of global warming. Energy-efficient technologies represent a vast potential to dramatically reduce atmospheric emissions of sulfur oxides (SO_X), nitrous oxides (NO_X), and carbon dioxide (CO_2). Focusing on electric efficiency is a highly leveraged approach. For each unit of electricity consumed, 3-4 units of energy have been consumed at the power plant. Furthermore, power plants contribute about one-third of all carbon dioxide and nitrogen oxides emissions from combustion, and about two-thirds of SO_X. But similar focus ought to be applied to energy use in transportation, industry, and in buildings of all kinds.

While abating pollution has typically been regarded as a costly venture, requiring expensive technology that often impedes industrial efficiency, energy efficiency affords a means of reducing pollution at a negative net societal cost, in fact a profit to society.

85

And far from penalizing industry, it affords a means for industry to be more competitive in the global marketplace.

Because of global warming even environmentalists are reexamining the nuclear option. True, nuclear power generation does not give off carbon dioxide. But the safety issues associated with nuclear power—uranium enrichment and transport, safe nuclear plant operations and security, decommissioning, and long-term storage of high level nuclear wastes—still plague public acceptance. And the role of civilian nuclear power in overall nuclear proliferation is arguable. All acknowledge the severity of the risks, and few accept these as inevitable for the fulfillment of our energy needs. Research shows that per dollar investment, energy efficiency can abate seven times as much carbon as nuclear power. Efficiency provides a far cheaper and more attractive energy alternative. In short, nuclear might be a valid option from a CO_2 standpoint alone—but we don't need it.

Energy-Efficient Technologies

Energy-efficient technologies such as more efficient lighting systems, motors, appliances, and windows reduce energy use dramatically without any change in consumer behavior. These technologies will also benefit our society by reducing energy bills. Furthermore, from the perspective of utility companies, these technologies cost less to finance for their customers than the cost of just operating power plants. Energy efficiency can therefore be profitably implemented by utilities, as well as independent energy service companies that make money by reducing consumers' energy bills. Furthermore, financiers are gearing up to provide a toolbox of financing mechanisms, such as shared-savings, to assist in the implementation of efficiency.

Energy efficiency will provide more disposable income for ratepayers, lower the capital requirements of electric utilities, and will provide a means of reducing the national debt while increasing the productivity of the national economy. In short, it is hard to find a more attractive opportunity that at the same time cleans up the environment.

Recent advances in lighting technology illustrate the broad potential for energy efficiency. By systematically employing state of the art lighting technologies and using only those technologies that are currently commercially available and cost-effective, it is technically possible to save over 90% of the nation's lighting bill. Since lighting accounts for about 25% of total electricity consumption, there is the potential to save approximately 21% of the total electricity used in the nation. Furthermore, lighting systems will be far more attractive, enhancing contrast and color and likely providing increased productivity in offices. Through improvements in lighting alone, it is possible to save more than $30 billion per year.

There are approximately 2.8 billion incandescent lamp sockets in the U.S., which draw nearly half of the total U.S. electricity for lighting but produce only about 17% of the light. In other words, incandescents are very inefficient light sources, giving off most of their energy as heat. Many of these can be replaced with compact fluorescent lamps (CFLs) which are four times as efficient at delivering the same prescribed light intensity. While they cost about ten times as much, they last ten times as long. For a typical retrofit a $15 lamp can save over $40 in avoided energy costs over its lifetime. In commercial spaces, avoided trips up the ladder (since the CFLs last so much longer) can provide benefit even greater than the energy savings. In many commercial applications the payback for these lamps can be less than six months, providing more than a 200% return on investment.

The environmental returns are equally impressive. Installation of a typical compact fluorescent will avoid the need for 570 kWh of power generation, and if replacing power from a coal-fired plant will avoid between a half and a full ton of emissions of carbon dioxide (CO_2) and about 10 pounds of sulfur oxides, as well as nitrous oxides, heavy metals, and other pollutants. If replacing nuclear generation, a single CFL will avoid the production of half a curie of strontium-90 and cesium-137 (two major components of high-level wastes) and about 25 milligrams of plutonium equivalent in explosive power to 0.4 ton of TNT, or in radiotoxity, if uniformly distributed into human lungs, to about 2,000 cancer-causing doses.

It is not surprising that the CFL has become a symbol of the energy-efficiency revolution. But there are many classes of retrofits. Larger incandescents can be replaced in many applications by high-intensity discharge lamps whose color rendition is improving dramatically. Fluorescent lighting systems that use better phosphors are improving their efficiency. Delamping is possible using imaging specular reflectors. Electronic ballasts use far less energy and provide dimming capabilities and better light quality. Polarizing lenses and diffusers are focusing light more effectively for required applications. Task lighting is being more fully exploited as is more carefully controlled daylighting. Also key to tapping the gold mine in lighting energy savings are controls. Scheduling and occupancy sensors, coupled with photocell dimming controls, provide fundamental efficiency gains by turning off lights when they are not needed. In most commercial settings, the typical lighting intensity of 2-3 watts/square foot can be reduced to 0.5 watts/square foot.

The same extraordinarily large gross technical potential for savings is also available in the use of electricity to run motors. Electric motors in the United States use the same amount of primary energy as all highway vehicles and three-quarters of all electricity used in industry. Electric motors consume about half of total U.S. electrical consumption. As the single largest user of electric power, motors and their associated controls, drivetrain components, and maintenance regimes hold vast potentials for cost-effective energy savings.

To date, most emphasis on increasing the potential for the electric motor stock has focused on two basic measures: replacing burnt-out standard efficiency motors with high-efficiency motors and installing adjustable speed drives on motors. By adding another ten measures to this list, such as proper sizing and rewinding practices, improving maintenance regimes, etc., current research has found that it is possible to save on the order of 44% of the total electricity used for motors. This translates into a savings of 22% of total U.S. electrical consumption or another $30+ billion annually. Further savings are possible "downstream" in the way energy is used for specific industrial processes.

Going after the gross technical potential for energy efficiency is much like eating a lobster. While it is relatively easy to get at the biggest chunks, equally rewarding and nearly as large in the aggregate are the many tiny morsels that one has to dig for! It requires systematic persistence! Improvements in the nation's lighting and motor uses will yield savings of nearly 50% of total electrical consumption; about $75 billion in annual savings. Further savings come from several important though not as obvious areas: water heating, appliances, space heating, and space cooling.

High-performance showerheads provide another illustration of the energy-efficiency revolution. They use 1.5-2 gallons of hot water per minute (versus standard 5-8 gpm) and can actually enhance the quality of a shower while providing the consumer with a $60-80 annual return (a 300-400% return) on a $20 investment. Furthermore, the showerhead will save water and if the hot water is electrically heated will forego the emissions of about 1,500 pounds of carbon dioxide annually.

Indicative of the embedded nature of energy use in society is the "standby" feature in most models of new televisions. While one would assume that a TV draws no power when turned off, actually most televisions draw 1.5-8 watts in the "off" mode, a feature that allows the TV to come on instantly. On an individual basis this energy requirement is small (only 13-70 kWh/TV/yr), but in the aggregate the current stock of 135 million TVs in the U.S. consumes 1.8-9.5 billion kilowatt-hours for standby readiness, requiring the dedicated output of a large power plant. Conversely, national appliance standards passed in 1987, which set energy-efficiency standards for refrigerators, water heaters, air conditioners, and other appliances, will save 22,000 Mw (equivalent to 22 large power plants) by the year 2000.

Most commercial buildings regardless of climate operate their cooling systems year round. This is due to excessive internal and external heat gain. Efficiency improvements in lighting systems and office equipment can reduce internal heat gain. Better windows which incorporate low-emissivity coatings to allow more natural light without its associated heat can reduce unwanted external heat gain. Through comprehensive building design, it is possible to bring the average total energy use per square foot of commercial building space from 120,000 BTU/ft^2 to 20,000 BTU/ft^2. If this level of energy intensity were applied to the 4 million commercial buildings in the U.S., some 57 billion square feet of floorspace, the savings would exceed $100 billion. While capturing the full potential for energy efficiency will naturally be more complicated in retrofits, new construction must adhere to the strictest standards of energy efficiency.

The building stock, like the national debt, is a legacy that we leave for our children and grandchildren.

Technologies for electric efficiency are being developed rapidly; performance is improving and costs are decreasing. Given today's state of the art, huge savings are possible. But electricity accounts for only one-third of total energy consumption in the U.S. The other two-thirds is used for transportation and to heat, cool, and ventilate buildings. The good news is that in parallel with the improvements in electric efficiency, similar gains are possible in these areas as well. And again, the three-quarters rule stands valid. Cars, for example, are available that are four to five times as efficient as the average fleet efficiency. Further measures to improve building shells bear similar promise, and squeezing out more productivity in industry through careful examination of process design also offers a large potential.

Innovative Implementation

Despite the virtues of energy-efficient technologies they simply have not saturated the marketplace. Demand has lagged behind the pace of technological improvements. In many cases the increased cost of a more efficient refrigerator or lightbulb is too high regardless of the compelling economic advantage over the life of the appliance. Building managers are often leery of new technologies, and architects and designers are largely unfamiliar. Manufacturers of equipment such as a clotheswasher or an industrial compressor with built-in motors often do not incorporate high-efficiency components, and the purchaser often wouldn't know it if they did. In some cases industries that run around the clock cannot shut down their production despite attractive energy-efficiency gains. And once again, folks still equate energy efficiency with conservation or an actual curtailment in services, seen as sacrifice. Consumer education is fundamental to the implementation of energy efficiency. In the near term, however, most consumers do not have the upfront funds to invest in greater efficiency, i.e., "I'll worry about that tomorrow . . . today I have to pay the mortgage."

On the other hand, utilities must take the long view. They only get back their investments (power plants and transmission lines) over the life of the equipment. They can afford to invest in energy efficiency for their residential, commercial, and industrial customers if they are given a fair rate of return on their investments. In essence, they can profit from sales of energy as well as sales of energy efficiency services. Utilities, unlike most of their customers, do have access to capital, and their close relationship with consumers provides an invaluable tool in filling the gap between consumer reluctance and utility need to make upfront efficiency investments.

Electric utilities can become energy service companies providing power where needed and energy savings equipment and practices where indicated. The utility passes part of the savings on in lower rates and uses the rest to repay the cost of the service. The process is well underway. In California and New England, for example, utilities are spending hundreds of millions of dollars per year on providing energy-efficiency services for their ratepayers.

Regulatory reform of the monopolistic electric utilities is changing the nature of the industry. In a growing number of states, utilities are being required to do least-cost planning: comparing the economic and environmental costs and benefits of both supply- and demand-side resources. For example, utilities must compare the cost of building a new power plant with the costs of providing the same capacity through the distribution of energy-efficient lighting. Competition from independent power producers is being encouraged by regulatory commissions; there is a wave of private power plant construction, just as there is a wave of energy efficiency being offered by independent energy service companies. The new chairman of Consolidated Edison expects that one-half of load growth in ConEd's service territory in the next few decades will be fulfilled by energy efficiency, and the other half by independent power production. In 1991, half of all new power plant capacity will be built by independent power producers.

Utilities and energy service companies hold vast promise as delivery mechanisms for energy efficiency. So do personal and corporate actions, and so does government intervention. Government standards for energy efficiency, such as efficiency requirements for cars and local government building standards, can decisively capture savings. But to date most government attention has been in form of energy subsidies to nuclear, oil, and coal. These three industries have enjoyed the lion's share of nearly $50 billion per year in federal energy subsidies. Not only do subsidies make energy sources look cheaper than they really are, but they tilt the competition between competing energy forms. In terms of "bang per buck," each taxpayer dollar that the government has invested in renewable energy and energy efficiency has yielded about 80 times as much energy as a dollar of subsidy to nuclear power.

New financing methods for energy efficiency are being tested. For example, energy service companies are offering shared-savings programs in which there are no upfront costs for the client. Utilities are developing least-cost delivery mechanisms with minimal investment and maximum saturation. Utilities have progressed from providing low- and zero-interest loans to offering rebates for specific products, and now to providing generic rebates for customers who can save a watt in any conceivable way.

Leasing energy-efficient technology is an innovative and successful implementation approach. Utilities are bulk-buying compact fluorescent lamps at low unit cost, then leasing the lamps to their ratepayers at a monthly cost less than the monthly energy savings. This scheme requires no upfront investment from the ratepayer and decreases electricity bills. The goal of Burlington (VT) Electric Department's leasing program was to distribute 8,000 CFLs in the first year. However, this number was distributed in the first three months of the program and the annual goal was revised upward to 30,000 lamps. Furthermore, the city water department, inspired by the success of the door-to-door effort, has proposed to piggyback water-efficiency measures with the electric utility's efforts.

The International Imperative

None of the efforts made to increase energy efficiency in the United States and in the "developed world" will assure a sustainable future if global energy consumption patterns and demographics prevail. In India, for example, the average person uses 2% the electricity of the average American. In Ghana only 15% of the population has electricity. Yet in both of these countries and in many more, people aspire to an American standard of living. An international form of rural electrification is happening around the world in areas where population is growing fastest. Naturally, electricity has many benefits.

Electrification can increase literacy which in turn can foster better birth control and ultimately slow population growth. Fundamentally, electricity can provide refrigeration for vaccines. But the North American level of consumption cannot be replicated around the world without environmental ruin and dire conflict over scarce energy resources.

Presenting the energy-efficiency opportunity in the developing world is a huge challenge. Encouraging the innovators, giving them the knowledge and tools to implement energy efficiency, is a responsibility of global proportion. But our first responsibility is to take care of our own waste, to set an international example of the energy-efficiency imperative. Nearly simultaneously we must provide technology transfer and realign international aid spending policies.

Conclusion

Through energy efficiency we can boost economic development and competitiveness, we can maximize capital productivity and minimize regret, improve environmental quality, and guarantee lasting energy security. These reasons individually are impressive and important; collectively they form an imperative for action.

Our energy future must be based on cultural development rather than the wanton growth that we have relied on as the indicator of well-being. Energy efficiency not only provides us with technical fixes, regulatory innovation, and a host of new financing methods, it provides us with a template of a model of a world ethic for resource efficiency, one that is congruent with the notion of respecting the rights of future citizens.

The good news is that we now know how to check environmental degradation caused by our thirst for energy resources in an economically viable way. We have energy-efficiency opportunities that will allow us to redefine our national energy strategy taking into account the environment and the future. The challenge is enormous— only belittled by the prize: the privilege of healthy and sustainable life on the planet. Far from seeing the marathon as impossible, we will soon find that the process itself is empowering.

Food and Water
for Eight Billion People

Chapter 8

THE TWELVE-MONTH GROWING SEASON IN ALL CLIMATES

by Anna Edey

Most of us interested in the problem of how to feed a growing world population today, and tomorrow, are already painfully aware of the severity of the ecological and economic crisis facing the world. We hear continually about disastrous droughts, erosion, acid rain, desertification, depletion and pollution of groundwater, and even about how upper ozone depletion will be decreasing the ability of plants to photosynthesize. Rather than simply adding to the mass of literature that already exists about the problems, I want in this essay to emphasize some of the abundant evidence available today showing that it will indeed be possible to provide plenty of food, in any climate, in any season. I believe we could even feed tomorrow's 8 billion people while preserving and improving the quality of life for both humanity and nature. But before exploring some of the solutions, I wish to provide a few facts about some of the devastating problems.

By the year 2020, only as far into the future as the '60s are in the past, the human population is projected to be over 8 billion, 3,000 million more than now. Yet even now several hundred million of the world's people suffer from intolerable levels of food insecurity, malnutrition and starvation. The so-called Green Revolution, which started out with such great promise in the '50s, has largely played out its cards as the chemical pesticides and fertilizers, sprinkler irrigation, heavy machinery, and monoculture methods it is based upon have gradually leached the life out of the land, resulting in decreasing per capita crops and food security.

Food production accounts for nearly 1/6 of total U.S. energy use, virtually all in the form of fossil fuels. That is the equivalent of almost 100 billion gallons of oil per year. We need not discuss here the inevitable tragic consequences—environmental, economic and geopolitical—resulting from our vast consumption of the world's finite supply of petroleum. **From tillage to table, America's food system is almost totally dependent on nonrenewable energy.** If we were to use all of the world's known petroleum reserves for only the production and distribution of food, using the standard American agricultural techniques and feeding the world's population on the average American diet, then these reserves would be gone in less than 11 years.

More than one billion pounds of some 320 different toxic pesticides are applied annually on crops and forests in the U.S. This counts only the active ingredients, although many of the "inerts" are also dangerous. Yet another billion pounds are made here and then exported. Many of these pesticides are so toxic as to be banned in the U.S., yet they are sold abroad, often without warnings of the dangers. They are applied by inadequately protected workers on food crops such as bananas, coffee, and strawberries, many of which are subsequently exported to the U.S. Many thousands of agricultural workers are thus seriously injured each year, abroad as well as in the U.S., while the general public is insidiously affected by eating, drinking and breathing the residues.

When modern pesticides were first developed in the mid-forties they did indeed seem to be a miracle cure against insect pests. However, it soon became evident that the offspring of insects that survived the pesticides inherited the resistance to the poisons, and the pest infestations would bounce back more virulent than before because most of the beneficial pest-controlling insects had been destroyed along with the pest insects. Thus we got caught in the hideously expensive cycle of continuously inventing and using new varieties of poisons to try to keep up with the rapid evolution of the pests, resulting in great damage to the whole ecosystem. Pesticide use has increased 12-fold in this country over the last 30 years, **yet the percentage of crop losses before harvest has doubled**.

Some pesticides become many times more toxic when combined in the food chain, in the soil, and in the groundwater. Moreover, some are more carcinogenic and mutagenic when tested on lab animals that are fed low-protein diets, alcohol, or anti-depressants, and recent findings show strong evidence that pesticides suppress the immune system.

Populations in cold climates such as New England are now almost entirely dependent on foods produced in and shipped from far distant growing areas for most of the year. In fact, the average distance that food travels from place of production to place of consumption is more than 1,300 miles. The storage and transportation of this food causes enormous depletion and pollution of resources. For instance, every gallon of gasoline combusted emits 5.5 pounds of carbon, resulting in 20 pounds of carbon dioxide contributing to global warming. Thus each cross-continental truck transport causes about 5 tons of carbon dioxide pollution. In addition, primary agricultural areas are experiencing serious non-sustainable stress on their resources as a result of overproduction. For instance, California is facing serious shortages of water as most of it is consumed by irrigation, while in Iowa over 40% of the groundwater is contaminated with agricultural chemicals.

Irrigation, often essential for successful food production, is mostly accomplished with overhead sprinklers. Travelling in the western half of the U.S. one passes endless miles of fields shrouded in the mists of huge sprinkler irrigation systems. The water, coming as it does from under the ground or from mountains, hillsides, and other surface run-off areas, carries with it dissolved mineral salts. Because these sprinkler systems use so much more water than is actually required by the plants—due to so much being lost to evaporation—the soil gets laden with more salts than the plants can safely absorb. Thus the ancient problem of soil salination due to irrigation is continuing to be one of the ways that fertile farmland the world over is being laid to waste. In addition, the use of vast quantities of water for sprinkler irrigation causes devastating depletion of aquifers, rivers, lakes, and reservoirs, and also consumes a high percentage of the energy required by U.S. agriculture.

Clearly, prevailing agricultural systems are unsustainable and destructive. Many believe our situation is hopeless—not, however, if we do what needs to be done. We must undertake a rapid—but not hasty—worldwide million-fold conversion to harmonious, sustainable, regenerative, non-toxic food production systems. Thus we could transform world agriculture within a decade.

Fortunately there are now many systems existing that not only fit the above criteria but are also economically superior to standard American agribusiness techniques, especially if we take into account the full costs and the long-range consequences. Following are a few examples, some fully functioning, some still in the experimental stage. Imagining such systems multiplied and evolved in countless variations around the world, we can clearly see the possibility of feeding tomorrow's 8 billion people and protecting the whole ecosystem.

The first example is Solviva Winter Garden, an energy-self-sufficient solar greenhouse that has been producing organic food commercially year-round since 1983. It is located on Martha's Vineyard, an island off the coast of Massachusetts. We visit this greenhouse under the worst conditions, on the coldest night of the year. Outside it is well below zero degrees Fahrenheit. After struggling across snow-covered fields against the biting wind and shoveling a high drift of windpacked snow away from the west door, we step in and immediately pull the door closed behind us. We find ourselves surrounded by comforting warmth, humidity, and fragrance. The inside thermometer reads 55 degrees Fahrenheit, like a balmy night in June. Around us are 30 angora rabbits quietly muffling about in their community dens. As we walk through the 100-foot-long greenhouse we see the moon and stars brilliant through the glazing to the south, illuminating the lush leaves and brilliant flowers growing in raised groundbeds and hanging growtubes, cascading from ledges, and climbing up trellises. We breathe in deeply the scents of tomatoes, sage, nasturtium, and living earth. When we arrive at the east end of the greenhouse, we peek into the chicken room where the 75 chickens acknowledge us with sleepy murmurs, their warm bodies keeping their spacious quarters a cozy 70 degrees Fahrenheit.

The next day it is still bitter cold, but the brilliant sunshine quickly warms the greenhouse to 80 degrees. The heat-activated top vents have opened automatically to prevent overheating. The sun, shining on photovoltaic panels, is making electricity to power fans and pumps that put sun-warmed water and air into storage to keep the greenhouse warm through even the worst cold nights.

The miracle is that this garden is thriving in the middle of the coldest, darkest winter without any of the thousands of gallons of heating oil or dozens of cords of firewood required by a standard greenhouse, without any of the chemical fertilizers and toxic pesticides generally thought to be essential for successful food production, and even without any of the huge quantities of nuclear- or oil-generated electricity normally necessary for lighting and ventilation. Yes, it is yielding exceptionally high quantities of the very finest quality salad greens, cooking greens, herbs, flowers, and eggs, continuously throughout the year, in both the coldest winter and the hottest summer.

The Solviva Winter Garden is a true solar greenhouse, heated free by the sun not only when the sun is shining, but even through the worst blizzards and prolonged cloudy spells, because of insulation and because the sun's heat is stored in masses of water and soil. Supplementing this is the free heat provided by the warm-blooded animals, the chickens and rabbits, at a rate of 8 BTU per pound of animal each hour. The other contribution from the animals, perhaps even more valuable than the heat, is the carbon dioxide they exhale. Heightened levels of CO_2 increase photosynthesis during daylight hours, tremendously compensating for the low mid-winter light levels, and the plants grow much faster than they would without it. The animals also provide manure compost for soil fertility, again free because they more than pay for their feed with the eggs and angora fiber they produce. Pest insects are controlled by harmonious insect management: introducing beneficial insects to predatorize and parasitize the harmful ones, and maintaining these beneficial insects by providing a good climate, a living soil rich in compost, and plenty of nectar-producing flowers. The key to success lies in not using any toxic pesticides, not even the mildest ones. This system is simple, low-cost, safe, and it works.

This greenhouse, brimming with perpetual vitality, even in the middle of the cold New England winter, is absolute proof that we can provide the entire population with plentiful, nutritious and affordable supplies of many foods without using up the world's resources, without polluting human or wild habitats, and without being dependent on foreign oil from the other side of the planet "secured" by hideously expensive and dangerous military might.

This greenhouse proves that just 1/13 acre can provide daily servings of vegetables, meat and eggs for 200 people all through the cold season. And furthermore, when combined with the 1/8-acre summer garden, plus some space for composting, the resulting 1/4 acre thus managed can generate an income of more than $100,000 per year, making it a very good livelihood indeed. By adding yet another acre, sufficient feed could be produced for the animals, eliminating the need to buy it. It is not difficult to calculate how many acres would be required, and how much employment would be created, to supply these foods for all the people of Martha's Vineyard, or Massachusetts, or the U.S.—or even the 8 billion people in tomorrow's world.*

Now imagine this greenhouse with some additional insulation and combined with a human dwelling, making possible an extended growing season even in lands with permafrost, such as northern Alaska or Siberia. Then imagine it in a place of the opposite extreme, such as Ethiopia. Because the greenhouse is so successfully self-cooling, it would work to great advantage in hot and arid regions, where food production is extremely problematic. It would provide protection from the scorching sun, insects, drying winds, and the occasional torrential downpours. Thus even populations in such marginal lands could develop their own local, reliable, self-regenerative, and plentiful food production.

The next example is derived from my own home which I have lived in since 1980 and call Solviva Solar Greenhome. Again let us

---

*These calculations do not include the production of other vegetables, grains, beans, nuts, and fruit, but current research shows that far greater yields are possible than the prevailing petrochemical mechanical agricultural methods provide.

Editors' Note: The author's figures, as noted, do not include the starchy vegetables such as beans and root vegetables, nor cereals and nuts. However, they do clarify the feasibility of adequate nutrition for 8 billion people utilizing the natural processes which have supported life on this planet for billions of years.

imagine a bitter cold and windy day, the landscape blanketed in deep snow. We step inside and are again comforted by that clean and fragrant warmth. The sun is streaming in through masses of ripening tomatoes hanging on 25-foot-long vines winding into the living room, kitchen, and weaving studio. It is shining on vibrantly healthy vegetables and herbs, through fragrant jasmine, nasturtium, sweetpeas, and even a coffee bush. While winter rages outside, we can pick incomparably delicious tomatoes and salad greens every day and sit in the warmth to eat them with no heat source other than the sun, our nuclear power safely 93 million miles away. The back-up heat source on cloudy days and cold nights is waste paper burned in a Franklin stove surrounded by heat-absorbing mass and water pipes. Thus space and water heating is free.

As in the commercial greenhouse, no toxic pesticides are used. But unlike the big greenhouse, where the animals provide the soil fertility, here it is provided by people. The subject of human body waste deserves special consideration, because although it is actually an excellent fertilizer and needs to be treated as such, and although it could indeed supply most of the fertility for growing the world's food, it is tragically wasted and instead causes massive pollution. Human body wastes represent the greatest taboo, particularly in the United States. This is understandable because of the long history of recirculating human disease pathogens through poor sanitation. Properly functioning flush toilets, septic systems, and chemical sewage-treatment facilities do reduce the spread of disease from human wastes. But the vast quantities of nutrients that are left in the effluent contaminate the environment, resulting in nitrates in the groundwater and algae infestation and putrefaction of surface waters. Deterioration of lakes and estuaries is generally blamed on agricultural and landscaping fertilizer run-offs and on ducks and geese. But knowing that each of us emits approximately 10 pounds of nitrogen per year and that this is more than enough to grow all the food required for an individual makes it easy to understand that in most cases the major cause of nitrate pollution is the vast quantities of nitrogen generated by a community of people. The use of toxic sewage-treatment chemicals compounds the problem, and the whole process represents a vast burden on the taxpayers that could be greatly reduced with biological sewage-treatment systems.

I know about the superior qualities of humanure as a fertilizer from 15 years of direct experience. In fact, it was the accidental discovery of the miraculous fertilizing power of my urine, diluted 1:10, that gave me the inspiration and faith to go on the quest for sustainable living systems. Now I am advocating that we solve two problems in one stroke: let us create fertility and tilth for our impoverished soils by converting our organic wastes into sterile fertilizer. Thereby we can reduce the amount of chemical fertilizers we manufacture and use by 75% or more, as well as eliminate the problems of pollution caused by human body wastes, predictably before the end of this century. The current laws requiring us to leach our septage into the ground (drinking) water will be recognized as utmost folly, and this will be reversed, instead permitting only nutrient-free discharge.

The composition of humanure is about 11% nitrogen, 4% phosphorus, 3% potassium, and 5% calcium, and whether from compostoilets or water flush toilets, it can be combined with the food wastes and other organic matter in our waste stream and converted into highly beneficial compost. In order to guarantee that this would not result in the spread of disease pathogens, every bit of the compost needs to be heat-treated up to pasteurizing temperature. I have achieved 170 degrees Fahrenheit from solar energy only, baking the compost in a simple solar hotbox, and therefore know that compost pasteurization can safely and economically be done even on a large municipal scale. Thus most of the fertility required for growing firewood, flowers, and food, even grain and beans for the people of any place on Earth, can safely be produced from the waste products generated by those people, saving money and natural resources, preventing pollution and generating local employment. Converting and using our human, animal and other organic waste products this way would reverse the enormous loss of topsoil and fertility that has resulted from decades of reliance on chemical fertilizers. In 1950 one ton of fertilizer yielded about 49 tons of grain. However, by 1980 that same ton of fertilizer returned only 13 tons of grain, and the yield per ton has been going down ever since.

The above examples of regenerative, reliable, plentiful, and nonpolluting food production systems are from direct experience at Solviva. Now, to describe some other proven techniques that help us understand how it will be possible to sustainably feed tomorrow's 8 billion people.

The first describes an irrigation system which in the future will most likely be widely used around the globe.

Imagine a village in an arid climate. All around are miles of dry, crusty, barren ground, marred by deep erosion gullies. A few scorched plants struggle to survive. Earlier attempts at American-style agriculture failed miserably as the sprinkler irrigation, chemical fertilizers, and pesticides caused toxic salt and poison buildup and massive erosion, while the dependency on expensive and unreliable imported fuel, chemicals, spare parts, and mechanical expertise ruined the local economy and the self-esteem of the people. But now there is a huge and thriving garden in this desert. In neat rows and groupings grow all kinds of vegetables and flowers, fruit trees and berry bushes, as well as grains; this farm is providing bountifully not only for the village consumption but also for trading. This agriculture depends on an irrigation system that is as simple, reliable, and cheap as the ancient traditional surface irrigation but is far more efficient and water-conserving than those systems or modern maintenance-intensive drip irrigation. Close to 100% of the water is available for the crops, as compared with sprinkler irrigation where often 75% of the water is lost to evaporation. This alternative system consumes no energy for spreading the water since that work is done by the natural force of capillary action in the soil. If groundwater is used, a low-energy solar-powered pump can be used to bring the water to the surface. This system minimizes the risk of soil salination, and bad water like sewage can be used to advantage safely and without costly chemicals and filters.

The CIT irrigation system consists of special ceramic pipes with an indefinite life-span that are permanently installed underground below plow depth. It was invented by Swedish innovator Bo Jufors who, sponsored by the Swedish government, has been successfully testing the system for several years in arid areas around the world. Grains, corn, vegetables, and fruit trees have been grown everywhere with excellent results. Not only are there enormous savings in water and energy, but the plants are also healthier and deeper rooted, and because the surface can be kept dry once the plants have developed roots, fewer weed seeds sprout, eliminating the need for chemical weed killers. Also, fungus diseases are minimized since the green mass is kept drier. These favorable conditions have resulted in high yields, in most cases double the normal, and in some cases 700% higher yields than with traditional irrigation systems. Both the production and installation techniques of the system have been streamlined, and CIT agri-irrigation companies are being set up around the world to meet the rising demand. This system is demonstrating the feasibility of reclaiming deserts and depleted agricultural lands, as well as preventing further depletion of water supplies and soils in all climates.

The next example of sustainable agriculture is at an experimental greenhouse in North Carolina where Mark McMurtry has created an extraordinarily productive relationship between fish and vegetables. The plants grow in shallow boxes in plain sand, while the fish are in ponds dug into the pathways, thus wasting no potential plant-growing space. Several times each day the water from the fishponds—containing various fish wastes—is pumped up to flood the plant boxes where the wastes are filtered out by the sand. Microorganisms that live in the sand transform the wastes and thus provide the nutrients that produce superb tomatoes, cucumbers, and greens. The water drains back into the fish tanks, cleansed and oxygenated, to greatly benefit the health and growth of the fish. This system produces exceedingly high yields of the finest fish and vegetables and could quickly be erected anywhere in the world.

By adding solar energy for electricity and heating to substitute for the oil and nuclear energy, this system could be non-polluting and self-regenerative. The fish food, earthworms, etc., could be grown in beds of composting municipal food wastes and toxin-free sludge and septage and could be sterilized by baking in a solar oven before feeding to the fish in order to eliminate the possibility of spreading human disease pathogens.

Editors' Note: The irrigation system Anna Edey describes can be made even more efficient through the use of desalinated sea water (i.e., free of all contaminants like rain used to be). Also, Dr. John Todd tells in the next chapter about the Solar Aquatics system he has developed, which has the capacity to fully reclaim all sewage and contaminated water. Like Anna Edey, Dr. Todd uses the sun and the microorganisms whose interaction created the terrestrial ecosystem in the first place.

From the experience of growing food in the Solviva Greenhome and in the Solviva Winter Garden, and from knowing of the experiences of others, I can safely say that any region can be self-sufficient in vegetables, herbs, eggs, meat, fish, as well as mushrooms and most berries and fruits. And it is clear that by using municipal compost fertilizer and underground irrigation enough grain can be grown in more regions of the world to satisfy even tomorrow's population.

Even cities can become major food producers. For instance, imagine the United Nations building in New York City. It is 72 feet wide, 287 feet long, and 505 feet high. By hardly even changing the appearance of the structure it could be retrofitted on the whole south wall and roof. The agricultural production capacity would be about 25,000 salad servings per week, which at one dollar per serving would generate a gross income of about $1,250,000 per year and would also provide 15-20 good jobs. In addition, such a retrofit would generate the energy equivalent of 60,000 gallons of oil annually. Then imagine the same applications on schools, apartment buildings, and office towers, on any walls or flat roofs that see the sun. Such applications would keep the buildings warmer in the winter and cooler in the summer, resulting in tremendous energy savings. Thus cities can grow substantial amounts of food, with tremendous benefits of better nutrition and air quality, decreasing the cost of living while increasing the quality of life.

The '90s will see extraordinary opportunities for designers and builders of sustainable living systems, both by retrofitting existing buildings and in new construction, for architects and engineers as they search for the most economical, efficient, and beautiful ways of harnessing inexhaustible non-polluting energy sources and biological processes, and for farmers to produce wholesome food without costly petrochemicals. Waste management companies could be providing customers with methane gas, electricity, and fertilizers generated from sewage and organic wastes. The power companies will be able to increase their profits and offer lower rates by harnessing the free energy from the sun through photovoltaics, not by covering thousands of acres of wilderness and farmland with photovoltaic panels, but by covering the collecting surfaces that already exist exactly where the energy is needed, namely the south-facing roofs in every community and city. By interfacing solar electricity and promoting efficiency the need for nuclear-, oil- and coal-generated electricity can be reduced by over 75%. Car manufacturers will sell vehicles with highly efficient engines interfaced with solar-powered motors. Even chemical companies, as they realize that there will be a drastic reduction in the demand for chemical fertilizers and pesticides, could find creative and profitable ways of funneling their productivity into better and stronger glazing materials, safer insulation and coolant materials, and fully recyclable packaging.

All human society, in whatever climate and whatever stage of development, will profit as the beneficial life-support systems gradually replace the destructive ones. People will realize that to live sustainably does not mean giving up cars or meat or long, hot showers and baths, but that instead there exists the distinct possibility of improving the quality of life for the whole ecosystem, ourselves and our grandchildren and their great-great-great-grandchildren, too.

Many believe that in order to have plenty of food and safe waste management it is essential to use ecologically destructive methods, and that to keep warm it is inevitable that we burn up our trees and oil and cause pollution. But contrary to this popular opinion, I do believe we can all "have our cake and eat it too," IF we do it right.

Chapter 9

LIVING MACHINES
FOR PURE WATER
Sewage as Resource

by John Todd

That modern societies are out of balance with the natural world has become a truism. It is my thesis that the contemporary technologies which support industrial societies are inadequate in terms of protecting the environment and dealing with resource scarcities and inequities between peoples and regions. What is needed is a fundamental technological revolution that will integrate advanced societies with the natural world to the mutual benefit of both. Pollution, atmospheric alteration, and the loss of soils and biotic diversity are artifacts of technological cultures estranged from the great natural systems of the planet. Modern cultures exploit the natural world and in so doing threaten their own long-term viability. It is essential that we create a truly symbiotic relationship with nature. This relationship will be predicated on new, highly evolved technologies I call Living Machines.* A living machine is a device made up of living organisms of all types and usually housed within a casing or structure of "gossamer" materials. Like a conventional machine it is comprised of interrelated parts with separate functions used in the performance of some type of work. Living machines can be designed

---

*I wish to acknowledge the insights of Barry Silverstein, who suggested the term "Living Machines" as being an appropriate description of the products of ecological engineering.

to produce fuels or food, to treat wastes, to purify air, to regulate climates, or even all of these simultaneously. They are engineered with the same design principles used by nature to build and regulate its great ecologies in forests, lakes, prairies or estuaries. Their primary energy source is sunlight. Like the planet, living machines have hydrological and mineral cycles.

They are, however, totally new contained environments. To create a living machine organisms are reassembled in unique ways for specific purposes. The machine's parts or living components can come from almost any region of the planet and be recombined in utterly new ways. The reassembly or building of the machine is based upon knowledge of the natural history and the niches of the organisms that make up the parts, and upon a calculated determination of their individual fit into a unique constellation of organisms reassembled by the engineer for a given purpose.

I have, for example, in my office an ecological digester for treating wastes. It was designed to eliminate pulp and paper wastes without discharge of waste material into the external environment. Normally pulp and paper sludge is impossible to treat and is disposed of in landfills. The living machine in my office is small, housed within two interconnected, thin-walled translucent fiberglass cylinders filled with water. Sunlight penetrates the top and sides. The internal environment is almost entirely bathed in light during daylight hours. Inside the cylinders is a complex of rock minerals, diverse algae species from New England lakes and ponds, and bacteria, fungi, and protozoans from local environments. There are also "manufactured" bacteria, molluscs from Europe and North America, crayfish from North America, and fish from Europe, Africa and South America. Higher plants from every continent except Antarctica are rafted on the surface or integrated within the system. The exotics in the system, like goldfish or carp, are either ubiquitous in this part of the world or incapable of surviving in the wild in a temperate climate. Examples of the latter include fishes from tropical Africa and South America and some of the floating plants like water hyacinth that cannot survive northern winters in the wild.

Within this ecological digester microbial life attaches itself to the wastes, a heavy gooey sludge which is thereby preconditioned for animals in the system. The microbes are protected by the gases, especially the oxygen produced by algae and higher plants. Toxic substances are also processed by photosynthetic organisms which, in turn, are sustained by organics solubilized by the bacteria. This living machine requires animals to function. Animal filter feeders and detritus eaters pass the pulp sludge back and forth through their guts and intestines.

The original waste material is digested and transformed into a wide range of byproducts, some of which are useful. The whole system is a microcosmos comprised of a large number of species. Its ecological engineering is global in terms of the selection of organisms but very specific in design. In the case of the pulp waste digester, it was the quality and characteristics of the sludge itself that dictated the organisms and also the ratios of the various organisms to the others. Initially a balance was achieved by trial and error. In order to optimize performance some of the original species had to be removed and replaced with others.

Over the past twenty years, with my associates I have designed and built a number of living machines to grow food, heat and cool buildings, and treat sewage, sludge, septage, and boat wastes. It is possible to apply the same ecological engineering to the production of high-quality fuels including hydrogen gas. Ecologically engineered machines can also produce byproducts that can be used in the manufacture of materials ranging from paper products to advanced composite construction materials. Linked living machines, which themselves form an engineered ecology of machines, can be designed to protect and even restore natural environments. They can also support human communities.

Living machines are fundamentally different from conventional machines. They represent, in essence, the intelligence of the forest or the lake, reapplied to human ends. Like the forest or the lake their primary power is the sun, and like natural ecosystems they have self-design capabilities. They rely on biotic diversity for self-repair, protection, and overall system efficiency. Living machines need not be small nor isolated from larger natural systems. Scale need not be an overriding factor, as living machines, like nature, are made from parts which fuse the "genius" of evolution. These include such independent qualities of life forms as repair, duplication, and feeding and waste excretion, dynamically balanced with the interdependent qualities of organisms like gas, mineral, and nutrient exchanges. The same design principles embodied in a cell extend to encompass the whole planetary biota. This allows living machines to vary greatly in size. I have designed a living machine to purify three hundred million gallons of drinking water daily for a major city, housed within a greenhouse-covered canal twenty-seven miles in length.

The potential contributions of living machines to the twenty-first century is enormous. They are dependent on fossil fuels for the manufacture of long-lived materials, but not for combustion. They reintegrate wastes into larger systems and break down toxic materials or, in the case of metals, recycle them or lock them up in centuries-long cycles. Living machines have the potential to help feed large numbers of people, particularly in urban areas, and this capability could address issues of equity between peoples and regions. Some of the poorer parts of the planet, especially the semi-arid subtropics, have enormous potential for living machines. The greatest reservoirs of "spare parts" are undoubtedly the tropics.

Living machines further have the potential to release natural systems from human bondage. By miniaturizing the production of essential human services, they would free wild nature to develop wilderness without human exploitation. This is significant in that the long-term survival of humanity may well be predicated on a dramatic increase in wilderness areas, which are the great repositories of biological diversity.

Living technologies are a recent occurrence, scarcely two decades old. The intellectual pioneer of ecological engineering is Howard T. Odum, who coined the term in his seminal book *Environment, Power and Society* published in 1971. It was he who set the stage for the articulation and creation of living machines. In the same year Bill McLarney and I built our first such device, housed within an eighteen-foot-diameter, translucent geodesic dome in a clearing in the woods on Cape Cod. It contained an aquatic ecosystem for the culture of foods. Tilapia, at the time a little-known fish, was the principal product of our primitive engineered ecosystem. By 1980 ecological engineering had been applied broadly and put to practice by a small but growing group of scientists. In 1980 in *Tomorrow is Our Permanent Address: The Search for an Ecological Science of Design as Embodied in the Bioshelter* by Nancy Jack Todd and myself, we compared ecological engineering with conventional engineering and argued that the latter as currently practised was not sustainable over time. In 1984 in *Bioshelters, Ocean Arks, and City Farming: Ecology as the Basis of Design* we attempted to articulate the basic precepts for sustainable ecologically engineered technologies. The most recent book on this subject, published in 1989, is *Ecological Engineering: An Introduction to Ecotechnology*, edited by William Mitsch and Erik Jorgensen, and dedicated to H.T. Odum. It is likely to establish ecological engineering as a legitimate academic discipline.

Compared to conventional technologies, living machines have many unique qualities. It is their aggregate characteristics that most distinguish them. People accustomed to seeing mechanical moving parts, to experiencing the noise or exhaust of internal combustion engines or the silent geometry of electronic devices, often have difficulty imagining living machines. Complex life forms, housed within strange light-receptive structures, are at once familiar and bizarre. They are both garden and machine. They are alive yet framed and contained in vessels built of novel materials, some of which are still in the developmental stages. Living machines bring people and nature together in a fundamentally radical and transformative way.

The difficulty many people may initially have on first encountering living machines lies in the fact that although they serve human ends, they have unfamiliar attributes. A comparison between living machines and conventional technologies, including biotechnologies, which are not living machines, is presented in the following table.

Living machines' adaptiveness and ability to protect the environment are due to their photosynthetic base, which is powered by sunlight. Although secondary sources of energy can and often are used for control and light augmentation, the uniqueness and economic viability of living machines is based upon their dependency on photosynthetically based food chains.

Living machines are built with parts that are themselves living populations, often extremely diverse and comprised of hundreds of species. A key attribute is that their components replace themselves

TABLE 1

A Comparison of Living Machines with Conventional Technologies

ENERGY	LIVING MACHINES	CONVENTIONAL TECHNOLOGIES
Primary Sources	The Sun	Fossil fuels, nuclear power
Secondary Sources	Radiant energy Internal biogenesis of gases	Combustion & electricity
Control	Electricity, wind & solar electric	Electrical, chemical & mechanical
Capture of External Energy	Intrinsic to design	Rare
Internal Storage	Heat, nutrients & gases	Batteries
Efficiency	Low biological transfer efficiency in subsystems, high overall aggregate efficiency	High in best technologies, low, when total infrastructure is calculated
Flexibility	Inflexible with regards to sunlight, flexible with adjunct energy sources	Inflexible
Pulses	Tolerant & adapted	Usually intolerant, tolerant in specific instances

DESIGN

LIVING MACHINES	CONVENTIONAL TECHNOLOGY
Parts are living populations	Hardware based
Structurally simple	Structurally complex
Complex living circuits	Circuit complexity often reduces
Passive, few moving parts	Multiple moving parts
Dependent entirely upon environmental energy & internal storage systems	Energy intensive

LIVING MACHINES FOR PURE WATER

Long life spans … centuries	Short life spans … decades
Materials replacement	Total replacement
Internal recycling intrinsic	Recycling usually not present Pollution control devices used
Ecology is scientific basis for design	Genetics is scientific basis for Biotechnology. Chemistry is basis for process engineering. Physics for mechanical engineering.

MATERIALS

LIVING MACHINES	CONVENTIONAL TECHNOLOGIES
Transparent climatic envelopes	Steel & concrete
Flexible lightweight containment materials	Reliance on motors
Electrical & wind powered air compressors/pumps	Structurally massive

BIOTIC DESIGN

LIVING MACHINES	CONVENTIONAL TECHNOLOGIES
Photosynthetically based ecosystems	Independent of sunlight
Linked sub-ecosystems	Unconnected to other life forms
Components living populations	Only biotechnologies use biotic design
Self design	No self design
Multiple seedings to establish Internal structures	
Pulse driven	
Directed food chains: end points are products including fuels, food, waste purification, living materials, climate regulation	

CONTROL

LIVING MACHINES	CONVENTIONAL TECHNOLOGIES
Primarily internal throughout complex living circuits	Electrical, chemical & mechanical controls applied to system
Threshold number of organisms for sustained control	External orchestration & internal regulation
All phylogenic levels from bacteria to vertebrates act as control organisms	
Disease is controlled internally through competition, predation & antibiotic production	Through application of medicines
Feedstock both internal & external	Feedstocks external
Modest use of electrical & gaseous control inputs orchestrated with environmental sensors & computer controls	Sophisticated control engineering

POLLUTION

LIVING MACHINES	CONVENTIONAL TECHNOLOGY
Pollution, if occurs, is an indication of incomplete design.	Pollution intrinsically a byproduct. Capture technologies need to be added.
Positive environmental impact	Negative or neutral environmental impact

MANAGEMENT & REPAIR

LIVING MACHINES	CONVENTIONAL TECHNOLOGY
Training in biology & chemistry essential	Specialists needed to maintain systems
Empathy with systems may be a critical factor	Empathy less essential

COSTS

LIVING MACHINES	CONVENTIONAL TECHNOLOGY
Capital costs competitive with conventional systems	The standard
Fuel & energy costs	Highfuel & energy costs
Labor costs probably analogous- still to be determined	The standard
Lower pollution control costs	The standard
Operation costs lower because of reduced chemical & energy inputs	The standard
Potential reduction of social costs, in part because of potential transferability to lesser industrialized regions & countries	Social costs can be high

as they wear out. The life spans of these machines can be extraordinary, lasting for centuries if housed within long-lived materials. They further have abilities to respond and change with variations in inputs. The task may be set by the ecological engineer, but if the living machine is allowed to develop immense complexities it will establish new biotic relationships not seen in nature, thereby expanding options of diversity. The organisms in the ecological digester in my office or at the Center for the Protection and Restoration of Waters' ecologically engineered sewage treatment facility at Providence have never experienced the constellation of relationships they currently do as part of living machines. These organisms have the potential to self-design new relationships if they are adapted to the new contained environmental conditions. There are further subsets of self-design. In the Providence facility, for example, there are four parallel treatment systems, each comprised of fourteen components that separate the raw sewage from the clear water discharge. The sub-ecosystems self-design differently at each stage in response to input variations in external factors such as light or to internal variations in the strength of the waste stream. These self-design combinations are dynamic and highly varied.

Another important attribute of living systems is that they are pulse-driven. Daily, seasonal, and sporadic variations stamp themselves deeply on the ecology. The background of pulse creates the ability and vigor of the systems to recover from external shocks, which is impossible for conventional machines. A living machine can be overwhelmed by overloading or by light deprivation, and in the process lose critical organisms and ultimately the ability to carry out the assigned task efficiently. But, even under severe stress, some of the internal circuits will continue to function, perhaps requiring re-seeding to bring the system back to its original task.

Control species within the systems orchestrate the overall ecology, but the ecological engineering is in such an early stage of development that we do not yet have a clear idea of whether there are control hierarchies, or if a threshold number of living parts is the basis of control. I have experienced organisms that upset control functions. In the pulp sludge digester, one very active species of fish was keeping the pulp particles in suspension and making the material unavailable for detritus-feeding organisms. Removal of the fish species in question fixed the problem. The life histories of organisms are the building blocks of ecological design. It will be essential to graft ecological engineering to a sophisticated knowledge of natural history.

Many years ago Bill McLarney and I found large fish of the genus *Brycon* in small upland streams in Costa Rica. These streams had little in the ordinary way of foods for the fish in them, which nevertheless grew to be sizable fish. We then discovered that *Brycon* could capture and then digest hard and inedible-seeming fruits that fell into the stream. Closer investigation of the anatomy of the fish revealed terrifying-looking teeth capable of shredding hard materials, and a long serpentine intestine that was able to digest tough materials. It dawned on me then that the world is a vast repository of unappreciated or unknown biological strategies that have immense importance for humans, if we can develop a science of integrating the stories embedded in nature into the basic systems that sustain us. Human destiny is linked to the natural world. Conservationists and preservationists honor nature and work to protect those pristine natural places that remain. But the survival of civilization may well require another fundamental step. It may become essential that we enter into the natural world and use its teachings to reshape and redefine our tools and technologies. Good farmers and gardeners have always had this kind of relationship with nature. With the unfolding and application of ecology in engineering, it is now possible to extend this relationship into a new dimension.

The idea of living machines had to wait for ecology. It also had to wait for the materials sciences to evolve to the point where energy and environmentally responsive materials could be made and manufactured cost-effectively. The containing vessels for the majority of the living machines I have developed need to be fabricated from lightweight, high-light-transmitting, flexible materials which can be bonded and waterproofed. They must be capable of handling a variety of stresses including high pressure and ultraviolet radiation. These materials started to become available in the 1970s. By the 1980s new transparent materials like heat mirror were created to help reduce radiant heat losses. The next step will be materials capable of changing properties based upon internal and external conditions. Such materials will borrow their properties from strategies employed in nature, perhaps as dramatic as that of the skin of some lizards. Materials that are "intelligent" are on the verge of being produced commercially. One such example is Cloud Gel, a film material invented by Day Chahroudi that becomes opaque when its interior surface overheats and transparent when it cools. During the day, under sunny skies, it prevents overheating without artificial cooling. Other new light-transmitting materials trap internal heat under clear nighttime skies. In combination these materials can regulate and optimize the climates needed by living machines to maintain climatic homeostasis. Structure and containment vessels of beautiful shapes that cover many acres can be developed through this type of gossamer engineering. The term bioshelter was coined to define structures that link these materials with ecology.

The fuel-dependent and energy-intensive processes we know today will be gradually replaced by responsive materials that house and contain various living processes. Widespread development of living machines had to wait for this convergence of biology and materials science. When Buckminster Fuller opened the radically new pillow-dome at the New Alchemy Institute in 1980 he saw for the first time a living machine housed in one of his geodesic structures. Turning to the principal architect J. Baldwin, he explained that the pillow-dome was the culmination of his own work, namely the marriage of his engineering and ecology. The pillow-dome was glazed with three inflated layers of Tefzel, an inert high-light-transmitting material developed by DuPont. The glazing was inflated with argon gas, which functions as invisible insulation. Buckminster Fuller understood the symbiotic relationship between ecological engineering and the materials sciences immediately and knew that it signalled a technological shift of real significance. He urged the DuPont executives to pay attention.

The question of whether living machines will be accepted is not yet clear. Economically and energetically they make enormous sense. They are already competitive for raising certain foods and purifying concentrated wastes. A commercial facility to handle the latter has been built by Ecological Engineering Associates in Harwich, Massachusetts. Because living machines avoid using hazardous chemicals and are pollution-free in operation, they are appealing to environmentalists. The greatest stumbling block to their adoption may be the inertia inherent in conventional engineering and the wide gap between applied ecology and civil and mechanical engineering. Some engineers, however, are beginning to train themselves in ecology and vice-versa.

The biggest blockade to the emergence of living technologies could be the very phenomenon living machines are intended to solve, namely, the estrangement of modern cultures from the natural world. Nature is "invisible" to many people in our culture. It is my hope that the aesthetic and emotional feeling that living machines can generate in us will yet carry the day. These machines can be made beautiful and evocative of a deep harmony that is nature. New economies wrapped in the wisdom of the natural world are capable of creating the future we all desire.

Section IV

Living Space
for Eight Billion People

Chapter 10

CITIES FOR HUMANS
TO LIVE IN

by Richard Register

Earth Day 1970 brought us the emergence of the environmental movement as we presently know it. Activism on behalf of the Earth multiplied many times over, laws were written, lifestyles changed—at least for the time being—and whole new departments of government were created as the Environmental Protection Agency came into being and the Solar Energy Research Institute was established.

What did Earth Day 1990 add to the environmental movement? Besides yet larger scale and a recovering of some of the ground lost in the 1980s, the greatest gains for the natural environment at this juncture in history are probably going to result from new insight about the human-built environment. A new theme of enormous importance and vision was introduced: ecological city building.

The traditional environmental themes have come to be these: clean up, abstain from destructive activities, and repair the damage. The theme introduced during the Earth Day 1990 season was this: learn how to build right in the first place.

The way we build out towns and cities is the foundation for almost all of our technologies and lifestyles: *The First International Ecocity Conference*, held in Berkeley, California, in February, 1990, was the first major forum acknowledging the necessity to rethink and rebuild cities and towns. Innovators and experimental town builders, "appropriate technologists," ecological activists, city government representatives and transit supporters, lawmakers, and suppliers of food and lumber to the city came from around the world to say, "We need a fundamental change. We need ecologically healthy cities."

Why: Because dealing with one small part without a conception of the whole is not enough. Example: There is a major problem with the automobile everywhere in the world. Some propose better smog devices and others suggest more efficient engines and higher mileage or electric motors. Yet none of these approaches get to the cause of the problem. If smog devices reduce pollution, and efficient motors reduce fuel consumption per car, per mile, what happens if more people want to drive? In fact, they do. While car makers in the United States, West Germany, and Japan drool over the prospects of selling cars to an economically revitalized Eastern Europe, and millions of people in poor countries worldwide identify car ownership as a symbol of progress and a democratic right for all people in a just world, the fossil fuels are rapidly being transformed from a geological layer under the skin of the planet into a dangerous, climate-changing layer of waste hovering in the air above the crusty epidermis. Electric cars require just as much energy to move a certain weight a certain distance at a certain speed against a certain resistance—that's simple physics. A battery is nothing more than a storage device, the electrical equivalent of a gas tank. Electric cars mean a vast multiplication of electric power plants. Do we really want that?

Meantime, developers, planners, city officials, and national legislators steam on, building an urban/suburban infrastructure that cannot operate without massive use of automobiles and trucks. Cities are thus being built for future disasters—which are coming true right now. What is supposed to happen when the petroleum runs out? The fuel is a petroleum product, the asphalt of highways is a petroleum product, the tires are a petroleum product, and every year the cars themselves are made of more and more petroleum-based plastics.

Wouldn't it make more sense to build so that automobiles would be optional equipment for a rare specialized trip, available for rent, than to build so that we can't imagine life without owning a car? If we did build so that cars would be needed only rarely, wouldn't that help in many other ways as well, radically reducing death and maiming in accidents, reducing wasted money and time, providing money for other more valuable pursuits, creating quieter, more pleasant, and ecologically rich neighborhoods?

The fundamental ecological lesson is that all things are connected in *some* way, with most things connected in important ways that have been overlooked in society's rapid plunge toward building whatever can be built profitably. No part will be much improved in our society that is not understood as part of a functioning, healthy whole. Thus we will not solve transportation problems with "clean" cars, small cars, efficient cars, electric cars—or even with public transit alone.

Transportation connects something with something else; it isn't an end in itself, though traveling fast and looking good on wheels might be a kick for many people. Transportation connects home with work, education, entertainment, friends, and an experience of both city and nature. But what if the destinations were close enough that they could be connected with a short walk or a bicycle ride? That can only come about if we build differently, if we build for people rather than cars, if we build for "access by proximity, not transportation." To continue building scattered single-issue areas—office district downtown and an industrial park thirty miles out there, with bedroom communities off yonder, each unit with a double garage—requires high energy, high pollution, high physical hazard, and land-paving of vast proportions.

So why not plan for "mixed uses" instead, with many social, economic, and even ecological functions close together? Hiring local is an important part of the solution, establishing satellite offices, telecommuting more, establishing delivery services so people don't always have to drive a car to go shopping, and having more transit and fewer automobile support services like freeways and parking lots. All these are parts of the "transportation solution" that becomes evident when ecological lessons are heeded. They represent a systems approach, a whole-city approach, and they imply a much healthier ecological future than dealing with just one part of the matrix in conceptual or policy isolation.

What we are really beginning to describe is a new way of building a complex urban culture: in balance with nature. It's a way of building that will require a fraction of the energy and produce a fraction of the social and ecological dislocation of the present ways of building. If we imagine the diverse, compact town or city—more like the traditional European town than the American sprawl development—with areas like the old American town square or Latin American plaza rather than the giant suburban mall surrounded by fifty acres of parking, we are beginning to imagine a far healthier urban structure.

Add to that a kind of town planning that respects a natural ecology and agricultural values, that restores or protects creeks, wetlands, shorelines, and rich agricultural soils, and establishes in-city gardens and orchards in parks and along streets.

Add to that new architecture, "mixed-use" buildings with shops on the ground floor and residences above, with solar greenhouses, rooftop gardens and, in denser areas, bridges between buildings, rooftop cafes, sports facilities, and other public spaces with views over the town and local region.

And add to this all the small things individuals can do to recycle, conserve, protect other species and protect natural habitats near and far away. Add all these things to an urban and town structure with diversity close together and we are creating a vision of a culture with cities that is also a culture in harmony with its planet.

In some sense only vaguely recognized today by the most advanced "ecocity" theorists, cities could even exert a healthy influence on evolution. Human beings produce bodily wastes that can, when treated properly, enrich the environment rather than impoverish or poison it. Kitchen and garden "wastes" can augment this human resource to create fertilizer for our agriculture. In ancient Chinese cities, there was a zone around the city of agriculture enriched by the city in this way. Natural creatures of many sorts could use this resource the way birds passing an oasis in the desert can stop for food and rest. As such oases might figure into the healthy changes of evolution, so too cities need not be destructive to life in the long haul and could even help. But, they need to be rethought and rebuilt.

Now in the late 20th century, we are seeing a great revolution that is setting the stage for the transformation of cities. Likewise, the ecological transformation of cities into ecologically healthy cities, or "ecocities," will help that revolution define itself and grow. It is a double revolution. One part has to do with people learning to get along with each other, has to do with democracy, human rights and peace, is centered in Eastern Europe and the Soviet Union, and is symbolized most dramatically by the crumbling of the Berlin Wall. The other part of this double revolution has to do with people learning to get along with everything else—that is, all the other life forms of Earth—has to do with ecological responsibility, should be centered in the Western world where exploitation of nature is especially efficient and destructive, and will be most dramatically manifested in the rebuilding of the human habitat, that is, in the rebuilding of cities, towns, and even villages on principles of ecological health.

In both parts of the revolution, the notion of human rights will need to be balanced with human responsibilities, or peace on Earth and peace with Earth will be short-lived. The central enterprise in responsible human conduct will be the keeping of peace and justice on one hand, and on the other, the rebuilding of virtually the entire civilization by way of ecological city rebuilding. On what should we spend the "peace dividend"? Largely this, or the peace dividend investment will soon be nullified since the present structure is unsustainable and, if it is simply replaced as is, will endure only a short while longer.

So how can the ecocity be built? How can the ecological rebuilding commence? The question of what kind of organization is required for the enterprise is answered by saying, "practically all kinds." Bottom-up and top-down, large-scale and small, decentralized and centralized efforts ought to all proceed simultaneously. The long-term health of the whole biosphere is the ultimate criteria, and so the results of the ecocity rebuilding project are all-important. There is a role for citizen action, collective and individual, as public moneys are spent, for example, to solve transportation problems by helping build housing near jobs as well as transit between existing destinations, and as more people decide to live nearer work or build composting boxes for kitchen wastes and recycle more carefully. There is a role for companies that build large buildings and energy-efficient railroad trains, and a role for small bicycle shops and hardware stores selling energy-efficient lights and appliances. There is work for national governments in establishing Departments of Ecological Development to pursue building and to support individuals, businesses, non-profit organizations, and local governments that build experimental new town projects or modify existing cities based on ecological principles. There is a role for city governments courageous enough to rezone for diversity at close proximity—"courageous" because any zoning once established is difficult to change, and such efforts, even if for the long-term good, are usually very unpopular with people benefitting from the established situation (especially if they happen to be wealthier and politically powerful).

At all levels and all scales, governments and businesses could join in with enormous imagination and collective resources. Research and development efforts and retraining programs could reshape industry and commerce to reshape cities, and in turn, be reshaped themselves as the cities are transformed. Car manufacturers and oil companies need not go bankrupt and their workers go out on welfare; they should become institutions that develop new ways to conserve energy, exploring renewable resources like wind and solar. They should be sowing profits into railroads and modest bicycle paths everywhere, investing in the complex natural-energy buildings, public spaces, and restoration projects that taken together will create the synergistic effect of future cities becoming ecologically healthy and socially and economically vital for all their citizens, human and non.

As we learn how tenuous and vulnerable so many of our material and energy resources are, we may discover that the most potent resource of the healthy future is none other than ourselves—we the people. There are natural alliances that have barely occurred to us, which can be made into powerful forces for creative change. Ecological rebuilding holds unprecedented promise because alliances are not only desirable but intrinsic to the approach. There is a natural affinity, little-recognized as yet, between the inner-city minorities and the outer-reaches friends of wilderness—both are concerned with poisoned and endangered species, though one is human and the others are not. If we need to rebuild, that means work for everyone, including environmentalists, minorities, business people, labor. Recognizing that cities are made up of every kind of person and that the cities' problems—and solutions—belong to us all is an acknowledgement that cities can be either the Titanic that takes us all down or the Ark that carries us to a better life. Just as people have occasionally shared in extraordinary social efforts to defend themselves against outside enemies, once we recognize the boat we're in, we might begin to understand it needs all our efforts in a very major overhaul—for the sake of this generation and the next, this species and all others.

How can you get started? There are several organizations working directly on ecological city building in need of broad support. And there are several key writings. And there are steps implied immediately in the above writing: live close to work, support increased urban diversity and density around neighborhood and city centers, help transform suburban bedroom-community sprawl into focussed real towns with lively centers and employment accessible near homes, support solar and other renewable energy technologies. In a word or two, learn and get active—the future needs everyone to figure out this problem, and the future will have a role for each of us if we seek it.

A final proposition: as Earth Day 1970 gave us many new ideas for protecting and repairing the Earth, Earth Day 1990 has given us new ideas for reforming our society for ecological health—*literally* reforming. Earth Day 1970 gave America the Environmental Protection Agency. Earth Day 1990 could give us, in fairly short order, a Department of Ecological Development aggressively helping to rebuild society in balance with nature. Among a growing number of us, the need for ecological rebuilding is understood. Now the vision has emerged and anyone can adopt and help shape it, thereby shaping the way we live on Earth and the prospects for its future.

Chapter 11

COHOUSING
A New Type of Neighborhood

by Kathryn McCamant and Charles Durrett

Dramatic demographic and economic changes are taking place in our society, and most of us feel the effects of these trends in our own lives. Things that people once took for granted—family, community, a sense of belonging—must now be actively sought out. Traditional forms of housing no longer address the needs of many people, and they find themselves mis-housed, ill-housed or unhoused because of the lack of appropriate options. This chapter introduces a new housing model which addresses such changes. Pioneered primarily in Denmark and now being adapted in other countries, the cohousing concept reestablishes many of the advantages of traditional villages within the context of late twentieth-century life.

Several years ago, as a young married couple, we began to think about where we were going to raise our children. What kind of setting would allow us to best combine our professional careers with child rearing? Already, our lives were hectic. Often we would come home from work exhausted and hungry, only to find the refrigerator empty. Between our jobs and housekeeping, where would we find the time to spend with our kids? Relatives lived in distant cities, and even our friends lived across town. Just to get together for coffee we had to make arrangements two weeks in advance. Most young parents we knew seemed to spend most of their time shuttling their children to and from day care and playmates' homes, leaving little opportunity for anything else.

So many of us seemed to be living in places that did not accommodate our most basic needs; we always had to drive somewhere to do anything sociable. Even if we saw a house we could afford, we didn't really want to buy it. We dreamed of a better solution—an affordable neighborhood where children would have playmates, and we would have friends nearby—a place with people of all ages, young and old, where neighbors knew and helped each other.

Professionally, we had both designed different types of housing. We had been amazed at the conservatism of most architects and housing professionals, and at the lack of consideration given to people's changing needs. Single-family houses, apartments, and condominiums might change in price and occasionally in style, but otherwise they were designed to function pretty much as they had for the last forty years. Perhaps our own frustrations were indicative of a larger problem: a diverse population attempting to fit itself into housing types that are simply no longer appropriate for many people.

Contemporary post-industrial societies such as the United States and Western Europe are undergoing a multitude of changes that affect our housing needs. The modern, single-family detached home, which makes up sixty-seven percent of the American housing stock, was designed for a nuclear family consisting of a breadwinning father, a homemaking mother, and two to four children. Today, less than one-quarter of the United States population lives in such households. Rather, the family with two working parents predominates, while the single-parent household is the fastest-growing family type. Almost one-quarter of the population lives alone, and this proportion is predicted to grow as the number of Americans over the age of sixty increases. At the same time, the surge in housing costs and the increasing mobility of the population combine to break down traditional community ties and place more demands on individual households. These factors call for a thorough re-examination of household and community needs, and the way we house ourselves.

A Danish Solution

As we searched for more desirable living situations, we kept thinking about the new developments we had visited while studying architecture in Denmark several years earlier. After numerous futile efforts to obtain information in English about what the Danes were doing, we decided to go and find out for ourselves.

In Denmark, people frustrated by the available housing options have developed a new housing type that redefines the concept of neighborhood to fit contemporary lifestyles. Tired of the isolation and impracticalities of single-family houses and apartment units, they have built housing that combines the autonomy of private dwellings with the advantages of community living. Each household has a private residence, but also shares extensive common facilities with the larger group, such as a kitchen and dining hall, children's playrooms, workshops, guest rooms, and laundry facilities. Although individual dwellings are designed to be self-sufficient, and each has its own kitchen, the common facilities, and particularly common dinners, are an important aspect of community life both for social and practical reasons.

By the spring of 1989, more than one hundred and twenty of these communities had been built in Denmark and many more were planned. They range in size from six to eighty households, with the majority between fifteen and thirty-three residences. These communities are called *bofællesskaber* in Danish (directly translated as "living communities"), for which we have coined the English term, "cohousing"* communities. First built in the early 1970s, cohousing developments have quadrupled in number in the last five years. Their success and growing acceptance attests to the viability of the concept.

Imagine ...

It's five o'clock in the evening, and Anne is glad the work day is over. As she pulls into her driveway, she begins to unwind at last. Some neighborhood kids dart through the trees, playing a mysterious game at the edge of the gravel parking lot. Her daughter yells, "Hi Mom!" as she runs by with three other children.

Instead of frantically trying to put together a nutritious dinner, Anne can relax now, spend some time with her children, and then eat with her family in the common house. Walking through the com-

---

* "CoHousing" is a service mark of McCamant and Durrett. All rights reserved.

mon house on her way home, she stops to chat with the evening's cooks, two of her neighbors, who are busy preparing dinner—broiled chicken with mushroom sauce—in the kitchen. Several children are setting the tables. Outside on the patio, some neighbors share a pot of tea in the late afternoon sun. Anne waves hello, and continues down the lane to her own house, catching glimpses into the kitchens of the houses she passes. Here a child is seated, doing homework at the kitchen table; next door, John reads his ritual after-work newspaper.

After dropping off her things at home, Anne walks through the birch trees behind the houses to the child care center where she picks up her four-year-old son, Peter. She will have some time to read Peter a story before dinner, she thinks to herself.

Anne and her husband, Eric, live with their two children in a housing development that they helped design. Not that either of them is an architect or builder: Anne works at the county adminis- tration office, and Eric is an engineer. Six years ago they joined a group of families who were looking for a realistic housing alterna- tive. At that time, they owned their own home, had a three-year-old daughter, and were contemplating having another child—partly so that their daughter would have a playmate in their predominantly adult neighborhood. One day they noticed a short announcement in the local newspaper:

> Most housing options available today isolate the family and discourage a neighborhood atmosphere. Alternatives are needed. If you are interested in
> - living in a large, social community,
> - having your own house,
> - and participating in the planning of your home,
> perhaps this is for you. We, a group of 20 families, are planning a housing development which addresses our needs both for community and private life. If this interests you, call about our next meeting.

Anne and Eric attended the meeting, where they found other people who expressed similar frustrations about their existing housing situations. The group's goal was to build a housing development with a lively and positive social environment. They wanted a place where children would live near playmates, where individuals would have a feeling of belonging, where they would know people of all ages, and where they would be able to grow old and continue to contribute productively.

In the months that followed, the group further defined its goals and began the long, difficult process of turning their dream into reality. Some people dropped out and others joined. Two and a half years later, Anne and Eric moved into their new home—a community of clustered houses that share a large common house. By working together, these people had created the kind of neighborhood they wanted to live in—a cohousing community.

Today Tina, Anne and Eric's eight-year-old daughter, never lacks for playmates. She remembers their old house with its big backyard. It was a great place for playing make-believe games, but she had to play by herself most of the time. Tina liked to visit the nice old man who lived at the end of the street, but Mom wouldn't let her leave their yard by herself, worrying that "Something might happen and I wouldn't know."

Now Tina walks home from school with the other youngsters in the community. Her mother is usually at work, so Tina goes up to the common house, where one of the adults makes tea and toast for the kids and any other adults who are around. She likes talking with the adults, especially Peter, who tells great stories. If it is raining, Tina and her friends play in the kids' room, where they can make plenty of noise if they want. Other days, when Tina has homework or just feels like being alone, she goes home after tea time, or she may visit an older girl who lives three houses down from her. Tina liked her family's old house, but this place is much more interesting. There's so much to do; she can play outside all day, and, as long as she doesn't leave the community, her mother doesn't worry about her.

John and Karen moved into the same community a few years after it was built. Their children were grown and had left home. Now they enjoy the peacefulness of having a house to themselves; they have time to take classes in the evenings, visit art museums, and attend an occasional play in town. John teaches children with learning disabilities, and plans to retire in a few years. Karen administers a senior citizens' housing complex and nursing home. They lead full and active lives, but worry about getting older. How long will their health hold out? Will one die, leaving the other alone? Such considerations, combined with the desire to be part of an active community while maintaining their independence, led John and Karen to buy a one-bedroom home in this community. Here they feel secure knowing their neighbors care about them. If John gets sick, people will be there to help Karen with the groceries or join her at the theater. Common dinners relieve them of preparing a meal every night, and their children and grandchildren can stay in the community's guest rooms when they visit. They are part of a diverse community with children and adults of all ages. John and Karen enjoy a house without children, but it's still refreshing to see kids playing outside, or to share with them the excitement of finding a special flower in the garden.

A New Housing Type

For Anne, Eric, Tina, John, and Karen, cohousing provides the community support that they missed in their previous homes. Cohousing is a grass roots movement that grew directly out of people's dissatisfaction with existing housing choices. Its initiators draw inspiration from the increasing popularity of shared households, in which several unrelated people share a traditional house, and from the cooperative movement in general. Yet cohousing is distinctive in that each family or household has a separate dwelling and chooses how much they want to participate in community activities. Other innovative ideas are also being experimented with—single-parent cooperatives and congregated housing for the elderly, with private rooms arranged around shared living spaces. But unlike these other approaches, cohousing developments are not targeted for any specific age or family type; residents represent a cross section of old and young, families and singles.

Cohousing also differs from most of the intentional communities and communes we know in the United States, which are often organized around strong ideological beliefs and may depend on a charismatic leader to establish the direction of the community and hold the group together. Most intentional communities function as educational or spiritual centers. Cohousing, on the other hand, offers a new approach to housing rather than a new way of life. Based on democratic principles, cohousing developments espouse no ideology other than the desire for a more practical and social home environment.

Cohousing communities are unique in their extensive common facilities, and more importantly, in that they are organized, planned, and managed by the residents themselves. The great variety in their size, ownership structure, and design illustrates the many diverse applications of this concept.

The first cohousing development was built in 1972 outside Copenhagen, Denmark, by twenty-seven families who wanted a greater sense of community than was available in suburban subdivisions or apartment complexes. They desired a neighborhood with a child-friendly environment and the opportunity for cooperation in daily household functions like laundry, meals, and child care. Today, cohousing has become an accepted housing option in Denmark, with new projects being planned and built in ever-increasing numbers.

Although the concept was pioneered in Denmark and the largest number of cohousing developments are located there, people in other countries are beginning to build their own variations. In the Netherlands especially, more and more people are finding that cohousing addresses their needs better than other existing choices. More than thirty such housing developments have been built in the Netherlands, with nearly as many planned. Architects, planners, and government officials from Sweden, Norway, Germany, and as far away as Japan and Nigeria have visited the cohousing developments in Denmark and the Netherlands, and similar communities are now being built in Sweden, Norway, France, and Germany. We have chosen to focus on cohousing in Denmark because of the depth and diversity of their experience, and because we believe the Danish experience is the most applicable to the American context.

In many respects, cohousing communities are not a new idea. In the past, most people lived in villages or tightly knit urban neighborhoods. Even today, people in less industrialized regions typically live in small communities. Members of such communities know one another's families and histories, talents and weaknesses. This kind of relationship demands accountability, but in return provides security and a sense of belonging.

In previous centuries, American households were made up of at least six people. In addition to having many children, families often shared their homes with farmhands, servants, boarders, and relatives. Relatives usually lived nearby. These large households provided both children and adults a diverse intergenerational network of relationships. The idea that the nuclear family should live on its own without the support and assistance of the extended family or surrounding neighborhood is relatively new, even in the United States.

To expect that today's small households, as likely to be single parents or single adults as nuclear families, should be self-sufficient and without community support is not only unrealistic but absurd. Each household is expected to prepare its own meals, do its own shopping, and so far as finances permit, own a vacuum cleaner, washing machine, clothes dryer, and other household implements, regardless of whether the household consist of two people or six, and whether there is a full-time homemaker or not.

People need community at least as much as they need privacy. We must reestablish ways compatible with contemporary American lifestyles to accommodate this need. Cohousing communities offer a new model for recreating a sense of place and neighborhood, while responding to today's needs for a less constraining environment.

Cohousing Communities in the United States

Since our book, *Cohousing: A Contemporary Approach to Housing Ourselves*, was first published in the fall of 1988, we have found tremendous interest in this type of housing from a wide variety of Americans. People of all ages, incomes, and lifestyles are attracted to the social and practical aspects of cohousing communities. We find they are particularly attracted to the intergenerational aspect of these developments. While affordable housing is an important issue, most people's primary interest is clearly the creation of housing options that provide a stronger sense of community than conventional developments.

To facilitate the formation of cohousing resident groups, we have created a series of workshops and offer a national, computer-based referral network. By the fall of 1990, more than seventy resident groups all across the country were meeting to plan their cohousing communities.

In 1989, we formed The CoHousing Company, a design and consulting firm to assist resident groups in building their communities. We provide services in the areas of group formation and facilitation, site search and acquisition, land development, architectural design, project management, and finance. The CoHousing Company works with groups through the entire development process, from the "Getting Started" workshop through predevelopment basics, design, construction, and finally on the ongoing management of the community.

The first American projects will start construction in 1990. One of these is in Davis, California, where a community of twenty-six town houses and a thirty-six-hundred square-foot common house is being built. In the fall of 1988, a slide presentation we gave inspired the formation of the Davis CoHousing group and caught the interest of a local developer and the planning commission. The Davis group quickly coalesced around the possibility of building on a three-acre parcel within the developer's new subdivision. The resident group met for two years of planning before construction began and hired The CoHousing Company to facilitate a participatory design process and to do the preliminary design.

To generate a design that responded directly to this group's needs, we began by defining the design program—the goals and criteria the design should meet. By dissecting the many issues affecting the site plan, common facilities, and individual houses, the group was able to build a consensus about the design criteria for its community. The site plan was developed in a group process using one-eighth-inch scale block houses and lots of construction paper. By moving the blocks around, the future residents could compare different possible layouts with their criteria.

The individual houses, of which there are three models, range in size from 800 square feet (two bedroom/one bath) to 1,050 square feet (three bedroom/one bath) to 1,300 square feet (three bedroom/two bath). The dwelling prices will range from $96,000 to $140,000—comparable to housing prices in Davis—including a portion of the common house and community outdoor areas. The dwellings will be owned as condominiums with the home owner's association overseeing management of the common areas. Well before construction

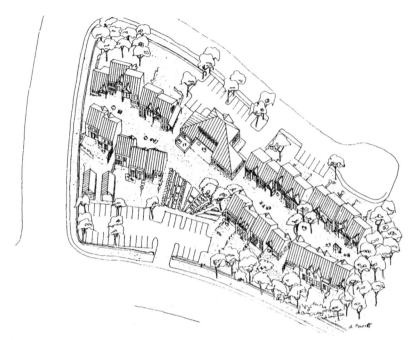

Preliminary sketch of the Davis CoHousing Community with 26 town houses and a 3,600-square-foot common house.

started, all of the units had committed buyers, and there was a waiting list for any openings.

Another project will start construction in 1991 in Emeryville, a former industrial area in the middle of the San Francisco Bay Area. We are converting a brick industrial building to a twelve-unit CoHousing community by adding a second story and doing extensive renovation work. Individual dwellings will range in size from 700 square feet to 1,500 square feet and cost from $122,000 to $214,000, again comparable for prices in the area. As a central, urban project with limited outdoor areas, this project is quite a contrast to the one in Davis. The group that has formed around this project includes singles, couples, and families and a range of ages.

The CoHousing Company is exploring the feasibility of several other sites in the San Francisco Bay Area including a magnificent waterfront site in the historic district of Benicia. We continue to work closely with resident groups, consulting on their group process and site searches. In Sacramento, for instance, we are consulting for the River City CoHousing Group which is lobbying for a downtown site owned by the Redevelopment Agency. Groups have also acquired sites and are preparing to start construction in Seattle, Denver, and Santa Fe. In short, cohousing communities are attracting the interest of many Americans, and the completion of these projects is bound to create even more interest.

We have already learned much about adapting the Danish cohousing model to an American setting, and we will learn more in the coming years. But we have noted striking similarities: When workshop participants explain their interest in cohousing communities, their comments are almost a direct translation of what we heard from the Danes. People speak of their frustration with the isolation of current housing options and their dependency on the automobile, the desire for a spontaneous social life that doesn't require making appointments with friends, wanting more contact with people of different ages, and the need for a better place to raise children. These words echo what we have heard from Americans all across the country—not just single parents and seniors, but also young families, professionals, and established homeowners. Clearly, many people are seeking alternatives not provided by the conventional housing industry, and some are ready to do something about it.

Section V

The World
of Our Grandchildren

Chapter 12

EARTH DAY 2030

Sustainable practices will have to replace the wasteful and poisonous ones of today if we're to celebrate that distant milestone with a healthy environment.

**by Lester R. Brown,
Christopher Flavin, and Sandra Postel**

On April 22nd, millions of people around the world celebrated Earth Day 1990. Marking the 20th anniversary of the original Earth Day, this event came at a time when public concern about the environmental fate of the planet has soared to unprecedented heights.

Threats such as climate change and ozone depletion underscore the fact that ecological degradation has reached global proportions. Meanwhile, the increasing severity and spread of more localized problems—including soil erosion, deforestation, water scarcity, toxic contamination, and air pollution—are already beginning to slow economic and social progress in much of the world.

Governments, development agencies, and people the world over have begun to grasp the need to reverse this broad-based deterioration of the environment. But what has resulted so far is a flurry of fragmented activity—a new pollution law here, a larger environment staff there—that lacks any coherent sense of what, ultimately, we are trying to achieve.

Building an environmentally stable future requires some vision of what it would look like. If not coal and oil to power society, then what? If forests are no longer to be cleared to grow food, then how is a larger population to be fed? If a throwaway culture leads inevitably to pollution and resource depletion, how can we satisfy our material needs?

In sum, if the present path is so obviously unsound, what picture of the future can we use to guide our actions toward a global community that can endure?

A sustainable society is one that satisfies its needs without jeopardizing the prospects of future generations. Unfortunately, few models of sustainability exist today. Most developing nations have for the past several decades aspired to the automobile-centered, fossil-fuel-driven economies of the industrial West. However, from the regional problems of air pollution to the global threat of climate change, it is clear that these societies are far from durable; indeed, they are rapidly bringing about their own demise.

Describing the shape of a sustainable society is a risky proposition. Ideas and technologies we can't now foresee obviously will influence society's future course. Yet just as any technology of flight must abide by the basic principles of aerodynamics, so must a lasting society satisfy some elementary criteria. With that understanding and the experience garnered in recent decades, it is possible to create a vision of a society quite different from, indeed preferable to, today's.

Time to get the world on a sustainable path is rapidly running out. We believe that if humanity achieves sustainability, it will do so within the next 40 years. If we have not succeeded by then, environmental deterioration and economic decline will be feeding on each other, pulling us down toward social decay and political upheaval. At such a point, reclaiming any hope of a sustainable future might be impossible. Our vision, therefore, looks to the year 2030, a time closer to the present than is World War II.

Whether Earth Day 2030 turns out to be a day to celebrate lasting achievements or to lament missed opportunities is largely up to each one of us as individuals, for in the end, it is individual values that drive social change. Progress toward sustainability thus hinges on a collective deepening of our sense of responsibility to the earth and to our offspring. Without a reevaluation of our personal aspirations and motivations, we will never achieve an environmentally sound global community.

Begin with the Basics

In attempting to sketch the outlines of a sustainable society, we need to make some basic assumptions. First, our vision of the future assumes only existing technologies and foreseeable improvements in them. This clearly is a conservative assumption: 40 years ago, for example, some renewable energy technologies on which we base our model didn't even exist.

Second, the world economy of 2030 will not be powered by coal, oil, and natural gas. It is now well accepted that continuing heavy reliance on fossil fuels will cause catastrophic changes in climate. The most recent scientific evidence suggests that stabilizing the climate depends on eventually cutting annual global carbon emissions to some two billion tons per year, about one-third the current level. Taking population growth into account, the world in 2030 will therefore have per-capita carbon emissions about one-eighth the level found in Western Europe today.

The choice then becomes whether to make solar or nuclear power the centerpiece of energy systems. We believe nuclear power will be rejected because of its long list of economic, social, and environmental liabilities. The nuclear industry has been in decline for over a decade. Only 94 plants remain under construction; most will be completed in the next few years. Safety concerns and the failure to develop permanent storage for nuclear waste have disenchanted many citizens.

It is possible scientists could develop new nuclear technologies that are more economical and less accident-prone. Yet this would not solve the waste dilemma. Nor would it prevent the use of nuclear energy as a stepping stone to developing nuclear weapons. Trying to stop this in a plutonium-based economy with thousands of operating plants would require a degree of control incompatible with democratic political systems. Societies are likely to opt instead for diverse, solar-based systems.

The third major assumption is about population size. Current United Nations projections have the world headed for nearly nine billion people by 2030. This figure implies a doubling or tripling of the populations of Ethiopia, India, Nigeria, and scores of other countries where human numbers are already overtaxing natural support systems. But such growth is inconceivable. Either these societies will move quickly to encourage smaller families and bring birthrates down, or rising death rates from hunger and malnutrition will check population growth.

The humane path to sustainability by the year 2030 therefore requires a dramatic drop in birthrates. As of this year, 13 European countries had stable or declining populations; by 2030, most countries are likely to be in that category. We assume a population 40 years from now of at most eight billion that will be either essentially stable or declining slowly toward a number the earth can comfortably support.

Dawn of a Solar Age

In many ways, the solar age today is where the coal age was when the steam engine was invented in the 18th century. At that time, coal was used to heat homes and smelt iron ore, but the notion of using coal-fired steam engines to power factories or transportation systems was just emerging. Only a short time later, the first railroad started running and fossil fuels began to transform the world economy.

Many technologies have been developed that allow us to harness the renewable energy of the sun effectively, but so far these devices are only in limited use. By 2030 they will be widespread and much improved. The pool of renewable energy resources we can tap is immense: The annual influx of such accessible resources in the United States is estimated at 250 times the country's current energy needs.

The mix of energy sources will reflect the climate and natural resources of particular regions. Northern Europe, for example, is likely to rely heavily on wind and hydropower. Northern Africa and the Middle East may instead use direct sunlight. Japan and the Philippines will tap their abundant geothermal energy. Southeast Asian countries will be powered largely by wood and agricultural wastes, along with sunshine. Some nations—Norway and Brazil, for example— already obtain more than half of their energy from renewables.

By 2030, solar panels will heat most residential water around the world. A typical urban landscape may have thousands of collectors sprouting from rooftops, much as television antennas do today.

146

Electricity will come via transmission lines from solar thermal plants located in desert regions of the United States, North Africa, and central Asia. This technology uses mirrored troughs to focus sunlight onto oil-filled tubes that convey heat to a turbine and generator that then produce electricity. An 80-megawatt solar thermal plant built in the desert east of Los Angeles in 1989 converted an extraordinary 22 percent of incoming sunlight into electricity—at a third less than the cost of power from new nuclear plants.

Power will also come from photovoltaic solar cells, a semiconductor technology that converts sunlight directly into electricity. Currently, photovoltaic systems are less efficient than and four times as expensive as solar thermal power, but by 2030 their cost will be competitive. Photovoltaics will be a highly decentralized energy source found atop residential homes as well as adjacent to farms and factories.

Using this technology, homeowners throughout the world may become producers as well as consumers of electricity. Indeed, photovoltaic shingles have already been developed that turn roofing material into a power source. As costs continue to decline, many homes are apt to get their electricity from photovoltaics; in sunny regions residents will sell any surplus to the utility company.

Wind power, an indirect form of solar energy generated by the sun's differential heating of the atmosphere, is already close to being cost-competitive with new coal-fired power plants. Engineers are confident they can soon unveil improved wind turbines that are economical not just in California's blustery mountain passes, where they are now commonplace, but in vast stretches of the U.S. northern plains and many other areas. Forty years from now the United States could be deriving 10 to 20 percent of its electricity from the wind.

Small-scale hydro projects are likely to be a significant source of electricity, particularly in the Third World, where the undeveloped potential is greatest. As of this year hydropower supplied nearly one-fifth of the world's electricity. By 2030 that share should be much higher, although the massive dams favored by governments and international lending agencies in the late 20th century will represent a declining proportion of the total hydro capacity.

Living plants provide another means of capturing solar energy. Through photosynthesis, they convert sunlight into biomass that can be burned or converted to liquid fuels such as ethanol. Today, wood provides 12 percent of the world's energy, chiefly in the form of firewood and charcoal in developing countries. Its use will surely expand during the next 40 years, although resource constraints will not permit it to replace all of the vast quantities of petroleum in use today.

Geothermal energy taps the huge reservoir of heat that lies beneath the earth's surface, making it the only renewable source that does not rely on sunlight. Continuing advances will allow engineers to use previously unexploitable, lower-temperature reservoirs that are hundreds of times as abundant as those in use today. Virtually all Pacific Rim countries, as well as those along East Africa's great Rift and the Mediterranean Sea, will draw on geothermal resources.

Nations in what now is called the Third World face the immense challenge of continuing to develop their economies without massive use of fossil fuels. One option is to rely on biomass energy in current quantities but to step up replanting efforts and to burn the biomass much more efficiently, using gasifiers and other devices. Another is to turn directly to the sun, which the Third World has in abundance. Solar ovens for cooking, solar collectors for hot water, and photovoltaics for electricity could satisfy most energy needs.

In both industrial and developing nations, energy production inevitably will be much more decentralized, breaking up the utilities and huge natural gas, coal, and oil industries that have been a dominant part of the economic scene in the late 20th century. Indeed, a world energy system based on the highly efficient use of renewable resources will be less vulnerable to disruption and more conducive to market economics.

Efficient In All Senses

Getting total global carbon emissions down to two billion tons a year will require vast improvements in energy efficiency. Fortunately, many of the technologies to accomplish this feat already exist and are cost-effective. No technical break-throughs are needed to double automobile fuel economy, triple the efficiency of lighting systems, or cut typical home heating requirements by 75 percent.

Automobiles in 2030 are apt to get at least 100 miles per gallon of fuel, four times the current average for new cars. A hint of what such vehicles may be like is seen in the Volvo LCP 2000, a recently developed prototype automobile. It is an aerodynamic four-passenger car that weighs half as much as today's models. Moreover, it has a highly efficient and clean-burning diesel engine. With the addition of a continuously variable transmission and a flywheel energy storage device, this vehicle will get 90 miles to the gallon.

Forty years from now, Thomas Edison's revolutionary incandescent light bulbs may be found only in museums—replaced by an array of new lighting systems, including halogen and sodium lights. The most important new light source may be compact fluorescent bulbs that use 18 watts rather than 75 to produce the same amount of light.

In 2030, homes are likely to be weather-tight and highly insulated, greatly reducing the need for heating and cooling. Some superinsulated homes in the Canadian province of Saskatchewan are already so tightly built that it doesn't pay to install a furnace. Homes of this kind use one-third as much energy as do modern Swedish homes, or one-tenth the U.S. average. Inside, people will have appliances that are on average three to four times as efficient as those in use today.

Improving energy efficiency will not noticeably change lifestyles or economic systems. A highly efficient refrigerator or light bulb provides the same service as an inefficient one—just more economically. Gains in energy efficiency alone, however, will not reduce fossil-fuel-related carbon emissions by the needed amount. Additional steps to limit the use of fossil fuels are likely to reshape cities, transportation systems, and industrial patterns, fostering a society that is more efficient in all senses.

By the year 2030, a much more diverse set of transportation options will exist. The typical European or Japanese city today has already taken one step toward this future. Highly developed rail and bus systems move people efficiently between home and work: in Tokyo only 15 percent of commuters drive cars to the office. The cities of 2030 are apt to be criss-crossed by inexpensive, street-level light-rail systems that allow people to move quickly between neighborhoods.

Automobiles will undoubtedly still be in use four decades from now, but their numbers will be fewer and their role smaller. Within cities, only electric or clean hydrogen-powered vehicles are likely to be permitted, and most of these will be highly efficient "city cars." The energy to run them may well come from solar power plants. Families might rent efficient larger vehicles for vacations. The bicycle will also play a major role in getting people about, as it already does in much of Asia as well as in some industrial-country towns and cities—in Amsterdam, the Netherlands and Davis, California, bike-path networks encourage widespread pedaling. There are already twice as many bikes as cars worldwide. In the bicycle-centered transport system of 2030, the ratio could easily be 10 to 1.

Forty years from now, people will live closer to their jobs, and much socializing and shopping will be done by bike rather than in a one-ton automobile. Computerized delivery services may allow people to shop from home—consuming less time as well as less energy. Telecommunications will substitute for travel as well. In addition, a world that allows only two billion tons of carbon emissions cannot be trucking vast quantities of food and other items thousands of miles, which is apt to encourage more decentralization of agriculture, allowing local produce suppliers to flourish.

The automobile-based modern world is now only about 40 years old, but with its damaging air pollution and traffic congestion it hardly represents the pinnacle of human social evolution. Although a world where cars play a minor role may be hard to imagine, our grandparents would have had just as hard a time visualizing today's world of traffic jams and smog-filled cities.

Nothing to Waste

In the sustainable, efficient economy of 2030, waste reduction and recycling industries will have largely replaced the garbage collection and disposal companies of today. The throwaway society that emerged during the late 20th century uses so much energy, emits so much carbon, and generates so much air pollution, acid rain, water pollution, toxic waste, and rubbish that it is strangling itself. Rooted as it is in planned obsolescence and appeals to convenience, it will be seen by historians as an aberration.

A hierarchy of options will guide materials policy in the year 2030. The first priority, of course, will be to avoid using any nonessential item. Second will be to reuse a product directly—for example, refilling a glass beverage container. The third will be to recycle the material to form a new product. Fourth, the material can be burned to extract whatever energy it contains, as long as this can be done safely. The option of last resort will be disposal in a landfill.

In the sustainable economy of 2030, the principal source of materials for industry will be recycled goods. Most of the raw material for the aluminum mill will come from the local scrap collection center, not from the bauxite mine. The steel mills of the future will feed on worn-out automobiles, household appliances, and industrial equipment. Paper and paper products will be produced at recycling mills, with recycled paper moving through a series of uses, from high-quality bond to newsprint and, eventually, into cardboard boxes. Industries will turn to virgin raw materials only to replace any losses in use and recycling.

The effect on air and water quality will be obvious. For example, steel produced from scrap reduces air pollution by 85 percent, cuts water pollution by 76 percent, and eliminates mining wastes altogether. Making paper from recycled material reduces pollutants entering the air by 74 percent and the water by 35 percent. It also reduces pressures on forests in direct proportion to the amount recycled.

The economic reasons for such careful husbanding of materials will by 2030 seem quite obvious. Just 5 percent as much energy is needed to recycle aluminum as to produce it from bauxite ore. For steel produced entirely from scrap, the saving amounts to roughly two-thirds. Newsprint from recycled paper takes 25 to 60 percent less energy to make than that from wood pulp. Recycling glass saves up to a third of the energy embodied in the original product.

Societies in 2030 may also have decided to replace multi-sized and -shaped beverage containers with a set of standardized ones made of durable glass that can be reused many times. These could be used for fruit juices, beer, milk, and soda pop.

One of the cornerstones of a sustainable society will likely be its elimination of waste flows at the source. Industry will have restructured manufacturing processes to slash wastes by a third or more from 1990 levels. Food packaging, which in 1986 cost American consumers more than American farmers earned selling their crops, will have been streamlined. Food items buried in three or four layers of packaging will be a distant memory.

As recycling reaches its full potential over the next 40 years, households will begin to compost yard wastes rather than put them out for curbside pickup. A lost art in many communities in 1990, composting will experience a revival. Garbage flows will be reduced by one-fifth or more, and gardeners will have a rich source of humus.

In addition to recycling and reusing metal, glass, and paper, a sustainable society must also recycle nutrients. In nature, one organism's waste is another's sustenance. In cities, however, human sewage has become a troublesome source of water pollution. Properly treated to prevent the spread of disease and to remove contaminants, sewage will be systematically returned to the land in vegetable-growing greenbelts around cities, much as this is done in Shanghai and other Asian cities today.

Other cities will probably find it more efficient to follow Calcutta's example and use treated human sewage to fertilize aquacultural operations. A steady flow of nutrients from human waste can help nourish aquatic life, which in turn is consumed by fish.

How to Feed Eight Billion

Imagine trying to meet the food, fuel, and timber needs of eight billion people—nearly three billion more than the current population—with 960 billion fewer tons of topsoil (more than twice the amount on all U.S. cropland) and one billion fewer acres of trees (an area more than half the size of the continental United States).

That, in a nutshell, will be the predicament faced by society in 2030 if current rates of soil erosion and deforestation continue unaltered for the next 40 years. It is a fate that can only be avoided through major changes in land use.

Of necessity, societies in 2030 will be using the land intensively; the needs of a population more than half again as large as today's cannot be met otherwise. But, unlike the present, tomorrow's land-use patterns would be abiding by basic principles of biological stability: nutrient retention, carbon balance, soil protection, water conservation, and preservation of species diversity. Harvests will rarely exceed sustainable yields.

Meeting food needs will pose monumental challenges, as some simple numbers illustrate. By 2030, assuming cropland area expands by 5 percent between now and then and that the population grows to eight billion, cropland per person will have dropped to a third less than we have in today's inadequately fed world. Virtually all of Asia, and especially China, will be struggling to feed its people from a far more meager base of per-capita cropland area.

In light of these constraints, the rural landscapes of 2030 are likely to exhibit greater diversity than they do now. Variations in soils, slope, climate, and water availability will require different patterns and strains of crops grown in different ways to maximize sustainable output. For example, farmers may adopt numerous forms of agroforestry—the combined production of crops and trees—to provide food, biomass, and fodder, while also adding nutrients to soils and controlling water runoff.

Also, successfully adapting to changed climates resulting from greenhouse warming, as well as to water scarcity and other resource constraints, may lead scientists to draw on a much broader base of crop varieties. For example, a greater area will be devoted to salt-tolerant and drought-resistant crops.

Efforts to arrest desertification, now claiming 15 million acres each year, may by 2030 have transformed the gullied highlands of Ethiopia and other degraded areas into productive terrain. Much of the sloping land rapidly losing topsoil will be terraced, protected by shrubs or nitrogen-fixing trees planted along the contour.

Halting desertification also depends on eliminating overgrazing. The global livestock herd in 2030 is likely to be much smaller than today's three billion. It seems inevitable that adequately nourishing a human population 60 percent larger than today's will preclude feeding a third of the global grain harvest to livestock and poultry, as is currently the case. As meat becomes more expensive, the diets of the affluent will move down the food chain to greater consumption of grains and vegetables, which will also prolong lifespans.

A Healthy Respect for Forests

Forests and woodlands will be valued more highly and for many more reasons in 2030 than is the case today. The planet's mantle of trees, already a third smaller than in pre-agricultural times and shrinking by more than 27 million acres per year now, will be stable or expanding as a result of serious efforts to slow deforestation and to replant vast areas.

Long before 2030, the clearing of most tropical forests will have ceased. Since most of the nutrients in these ecosystems are held in the leaves and biomass of the vegetation rather than in the soil, only activities that preserve the forest canopy are sustainable. While it is impossible to say how much virgin tropical forest would remain in 2030 if sustainability is achieved, certainly the rate of deforestation will have had to slow dramatically by the end of this decade. Soon thereafter it will come to a halt.

Efforts to identify and protect unique parcels of forest will probably have led to a widely dispersed network of preserves. But a large portion of tropical forests still standing in 2030 will be exploited in a variety of benign ways by people living in and around them. Hundreds of "extractive reserves" will exist, areas in which local people harvest rubber, resins, nuts, fruits, medicines, and other forest products.

Efforts to alleviate the fuel wood crisis in developing countries, to reduce flooding and landslides in hilly regions, and to slow the buildup of carbon dioxide may spur the planting of an additional 500 million acres or so of trees. Many of these plantings will be on private farms as part of agroforestry systems, but plantations may also have an expanded role. Cities and villages will turn to managed woodlands on their outskirts to contribute fuel for heating, cooking, and electricity. This wood will substitute for some portion of coal and oil use and, since harvested on a sustained-yield basis, will make no net contribution of carbon dioxide to the atmosphere.

Restoring and stabilizing the biological resource base by 2030 depends on a pattern of land ownership and use far more equitable than today's. Much of the degradation now occurring stems from the heavily skewed distribution of land that, along with population growth, pushes poor people into ever more marginal environments. Stewardship requires that people have plots large enough to sustain their families without abusing the land, access to means of using the land productively, and the right to pass it on to their children.

No matter what technologies come along, the biochemical process of photosynthesis, carried out by green plants, will remain the

154

basis for meeting many human needs, and its efficiency can only be marginally improved. Given that humanity already appropriates an estimated 40 percent of the earth's annual photosynthetic product on land, the urgency of slowing the growth in human numbers is obvious. The sooner societies stabilize their populations, the greater will be their opportunities for achieving equitable and stable patterns of land use that can meet their needs indefinitely.

Economic Progress in a New Light

The fundamental changes that are needed in energy, forestry, agriculture, and other physical systems cannot occur without corresponding shifts in social, economic, and moral character. During the transition to sustainability, political leaders and citizens alike will be forced to reevaluate their goals and aspirations and to adjust to a new set of principles that have at their core the welfare of future generations.

Shifts in employment will be among the most visible as the transition gets under way. Moving from fossil fuels to a diverse set of renewable energy sources, extracting fewer materials from the earth and recycling more, and revamping farming and forestry practices will greatly expand opportunities in new areas. Job losses in coal mining, auto production, and metals prospecting will be offset by gains in the manufacture and sale of photovoltaic solar cells, wind turbines, bicycles, mass transit equipment, and a host of technologies for recycling materials.

Since planned obsolescence will itself be obsolete in a sustainable society, a far greater share of workers will be employed in repair, maintenance, and recycling activities than in the extraction of virgin materials and production of new goods.

Wind prospectors, energy-efficiency auditors, and solar architects will be among the professions booming from the shift to a highly efficient, renewable-energy economy. Numbering in the hundreds of thousands today, jobs in these fields may collectively total in the millions worldwide within a few decades. Opportunities in forestry will expand markedly.

As the transition to a more environmentally sensitive economy progresses, sustainability will gradually eclipse growth as the focus of economic policy making. Over the next few decades, government policies will encourage investments that promote stability and endurance at the expense of those that simply expand short-term production.

As a yardstick of progress, the gross national product (GNP) will be seen as a bankrupt indicator. By measuring flows of goods and services, GNP undervalues the qualities a sustainable society strives for, such as durability and resource protection, and overvalues planned obsolescence and waste. The pollution caused by a coal-burning power plant, for instance, raises GNP by requiring expenditures on lung disease treatment and the purchase of a scrubber to control emissions. Yet society would be far better off if power were generated in ways that did not pollute the air in the first place.

National military budgets in a sustainable world will be a small fraction of what they are today. Moreover, sustainability cannot be achieved without a massive shift of resources from military endeavors into energy efficiency, soil conservation, tree planting, family planning, and other needed development activities. Rather than maintaining large defense establishments, governments may come to rely on a strengthened U.N. peacekeeping force.

A New Set of Values

Movement toward a lasting society cannot occur without a transformation of individual priorities and values. Throughout the ages, philosophers and religious leaders have denounced materialism as a path to human fulfillment. Yet societies across the ideological spectrum have persisted in equating quality of life with increased consumption.

Because of the strain on resources it creates, materialism simply cannot survive the transition to a sustainable world. As public understanding of the need to adopt simpler and less consumptive lifestyles spreads, it will become unfashionable to own fancy new cars, clothes, and the latest electronic devices. The potential benefits of unleashing the human energy now devoted to producing, advertising, buying, consuming, and discarding material goods are enormous.

As the amassing of personal and national wealth becomes less of a goal, the gap between haves and have-nots will gradually close,

156

eliminating many societal tensions. Ideological differences may fade as well, as nations adopt sustainability as a common cause, and as they come to recognize that achieving it requires a shared set of values that includes democratic principles, freedom to innovate, respect for human rights, and acceptance of diversity. With the cooperative tasks involved in repairing the earth so many and so large, the idea of waging war could become an anachronism.

The task of building a sustainable society is an enormous one that will take decades rather than years. Indeed, it is an undertaking that will easily absorb the energies that during the past 40 years have been devoted to the Cold War. The reward in the year 2030 could be an Earth Day with something to celebrate: the achievement of a society in balance with the resources that support it, instead of one that destroys the underpinnings of its future.

Appendixes

CALIFORNIA ENERGY COMMISSION PRESENTATION ON AUTOMOBILE LIABILITY INSURANCE

June 18, 1990
by Paul Rothkrug

The motor vehicle casualty insurance industry pays out 50-60% of its collected premium in the form of claims. Let's say 55%. Another 15% is spent investigating and defending claims. The rest goes into overhead, brokers' commissions, profits and reserves. The reserve component is for the protection of the claimant, but he never sees the money.

The claimant's lawyers get a very substantial portion of the claim settlement, up to 50% in a number of cases. Let's say it averages out at 15% of the premium.

The claimant as often as not has to go to court, spend time away from his job, and incur other inconveniences and costs which add up to about 5% more.

If we add the 45% retained by the carrier, the 15% going to the lawyer, the 5% of personal costs to the claimant, we find that 35% of premiums paid are returned by the automobile liability system to the public in the form of net claims paid.

There's another social cost involved which impacts the motor vehicle owner in the form of taxes. Our courts are swamped by the vast amount of litigation stemming from the use of motor vehicles. That cost is not only the salaries of the judges, police, government attorneys, and all the other expenses involved with our cumbersome legal system; it's also the price of the delay before the claimant finally gets his money. Between the taxes needed to support the court system and the cost of the delay, we could take another 5%.

So between actual costs and social costs, the insuring public gets back about 30¢ on each dollar of premium paid to the motor vehicle liability insurance industry.

The main social problem presented by automobile liability insurance is that we are attempting to handle the cost of automobile accidents through the common law concept of "tort," a French word meaning "wrong." This evolved in England in the Middle Ages to cover the damage done when Farmer Brown's pigs invaded Farmer Jones' cabbage patch.

The lever we propose to use comes at the problem from two directions:

1. A system of compensation for accident damages based upon the workers' compensation system, which has been in effect since the second decade of this century, with enormously beneficial social results all around.

2. The payment of insurance premiums to the state by the insuring public in the form of an insurance tax at the gas pump for each gallon of gasoline used.

In terms of claims paid to claimants as a percentage of premium paid, the workers' compensation is remarkably more efficient. Instead of the 30% we're talking about for the automobile premium, it runs more like 80%.

Workers' compensation allows a claimant to go outside the system, hire a lawyer and go to court, if they so choose. In point of fact, it's very much the exception, as compared to the rule in the case of automobile insurance.

The same privilege would be allowed the automobile claimant and it is anticipated that if the compensation system is equitable, the same low percentage of claims would wind up in court as is the case with workers' compensation, i.e., under 3%.

There are 145 million motor vehicles in the United States with annual liability premiums averaging from around $500 on the family car to something in the thousands for freight-hauling trucks and passenger buses. Let's say $700 per year per vehicle. This gives an annual insurance premium paid to the liability carriers of:

$101.5 billion.

At 80% efficiency instead of 30%, the following benefits accrue to society:

1. $50.75 billion.
2. Less time, money and effort wasted in court by literally millions of people who can now put more effort into socially productive areas.

Proposition 103, passed by referendum in the state of California in 1988, called for a 20% reduction in automobile liability premiums.

We can achieve that result if we pass 40% of the $50-75 billion saved back to the insuring public, say $20 billion. Society now finds $31 billion annually to ease the transitional discomfort of the motor vehicle complex of industries as they are prodded toward greater energy efficiency and environmentally healthier products.

We've already assumed a $700 average annual liability premium covering all motor vehicles from the family car to big trucks and buses.

If we make a further assumption of 15,000 miles of annual travel per vehicle and fourteen miles per gallon of travel (again including trucks and buses), we come up with a figure of 75¢ per gallon of gasoline as the approximate current cost for liability insurance for all vehicles.

Fifty percent of that cost can be recovered as discussed above (i.e., the difference between 80% efficiency of the workers' comp program in terms of payout to premium and 30% for the current automobile liability system), then the real cost of insurance per gallon of gasoline for the average vehicle is 37.5¢, and we have a savings of another 37.5¢ to distribute.

If we give 40% of the savings back to the vehicle owner, then the per gallon price of liability insurance comes to less than 60¢.

If we then arrange to pay for automobile liability insurance at the gas pump, even though the motorist is ahead since he has no liability premiums to pay, he's looking at an increase in the average price of gasoline of 60¢.

However, the driver goes to the gas pump a lot more often than he writes checks for his liability premium, so has a constant reminder that the less gasoline he uses the better off he'll be.

Thus, by translating the cost of liability insurance into a price per gallon at the gasoline pump, we have a constant encouragement to a more efficient use of the automobile, and a search for a more efficient fuel, giving yet a further incentive to the development of energy-effective and less polluting vehicles.

Differential rates would also apply by class of vehicle based on horse power, mean gross loaded weight and other relevant factors affecting mileage per gallon of fuel.

A magnetic strip on the driver's license to be run through a checking unit on line to the motor vehicle department computer would tell the attendant at the pump the customer's rating. The gas pump could be tied in to the electrical circuit with the checking equipment, to prevent gas from being pumped before a valid license is put through the unit.

Nationally the percentage of uninsured automobiles is estimated at from 16 to 30. Payment at the pump will relieve the premium-paying public of that burden.

This program will also release some billions of insurance company "reserves" (also known as untaxed profits) because the insurance industry function now becomes pure administration. The profits on the released reserves become a one-time windfall to the tax collector.

We have purposely not included collision damage in our proposal.

From a social point of view, we are not concerned with the cost of collision to the individual vehicle. The price of collision damage is directly related to the cost of the automobile and in practice the costlier the automobile the less efficient it is in terms of energy conservation.

Therefore, the higher the cost of collision insurance the higher should become the average motorist's concern with efficiency and safety in the design of his automobile.

Just as Medicare claims are paid by private health insurance carriers with funds drawn on the Social Security Administration, so will the liability insurance industry continue to handle the administration of the restructured program.

A motorist having a valid license and registration requests a policy from a licensed broker. There is no point in his not asking for a policy; he's paying for it at the gas pump anyway.

The broker (for a 2% service fee) passes the request on to a carrier, who mails a certificate directly to the motorist. Two percent is about all the broker now nets from the average automobile liability policy.

Claims are handled by the administrative carrier in accordance with the statutory provisions as to compensation for:

- medical expenses
- permanent injury
- loss of life
- property damage
- loss of time

The carrier does everything it used to do, except that it is now off the risk. The 20% administrative fee (less 2% to the broker) would be at least as much as they now keep.

The integrity of the program in terms of legitimate claims payments will be about the same as for Medicare (upwards of 95%).

The integrity of the program also requires an incentive in the price paid for insurance at the gas pump. This is in order to differentiate between drivers as to their respective records. Drivers could be classified A-B-C-D with A drivers getting a 10¢ discount, B drivers standard, C and D 10¢ and 20¢ penalty, respectively.

The Legal Profession

Lawyers, judges, process servers, court employees, bondsmen and the like will be released to provide services of true social value.

Lawyers, particularly, can have the opportunity to use their skills of communication and due process throughout the transition period.

The courts will reduce their case backlog to the point where justice would be better served.

The Automobile Industry

During the transition period and perhaps beyond, we will need two different forms of motor vehicles:

- low performance but highly efficient models for use in "metro areas" of one million population or over.

165

• higher performance but less efficient models for over-the-road travel, both passenger and freight.

City dwellers will own low-performance, high-efficiency cars. When they want to travel intercity, they go to a transfer garage at the city limits. There they rent an over-the-road car and leave the city car. When returning from the trip, they reverse the process at the city limits and travel home in their nonpolluting vehicle. Country and outer suburban residents will do the opposite.

The same procedure will hold for freight haulers.

Efficiency incentives are vitally important to large cargo trucks and buses. Transportation costs are a substantial factor in cost of living, and therefore in our competitive position as a society world-wide.

It has been our basic lack of concern with efficiency as a society which is resulting in the decline of our international competitive position.

Mass transit is a glaring example, with major relevance to the present discussion.

Mass Transit in Metropolitan Areas

This is a situation which must be handled simultaneously from the point of view of both improving service, and getting people out of their cars to use the improved service.

That our automobile commuters accept:

• up to four hours daily in their cars
• sitting through gridlock
• paying exorbitant parking fees and tolls
• breathing exhaust fumes for one-third of their waking hours

is testimony only to the deplorable state of our metropolitan mass transit facilities.

One major exception is the Washington, D.C., Metro now transporting tens of thousands into the District daily with speed and comfort. At suburban Metro stops we find vast free parking facilities for inbound commuters to leave their cars and pick them up again in the evening. Also "kiss and ride" areas where spouses can drop the commuters off and meet them at the end of the day.

If the United States Congress, the true government of the District of Columbia, can approve such a program for the nation's capital, surely part of the funds released from the shrinking defense budget can go into the kind of mass transit which will make sense to motorists, thus limiting the use of private automobile for urban commuting.

California's share of the reduced cost of liability insurance would be approximately $7,200,000,000.

With 40% going to the insuring public the state would have over $4,000,000,000 annually to:

1. Improve mass transit.
2. Work with the automobile industry to provide more efficient vehicles.

Our objective would be to increase average miles per gallon from around 19 to 40 at a gasoline saving of 7,000,000,000 gallons annually.

We could encourage the automobile industry by advertising worldwide for competent auto people to set up a prototype factory to produce 40 mpg vehicles, with other specifications, such as lightweight batteries for use in metropolitan areas and so forth.

If California used half of its $4 billion share of the insurance savings for mass transit, the remaining half would be sufficient to provide each purchaser of the new vehicles with a $1,600 subsidy to the trade-in value of the old one. At the point where production of the new vehicles reaches the annual replacement demand, we could provide that no further old-style ones will be allowed into the state.

Beyond that, consumer savings for the purchase of gasoline and insurance in California will be close to 10 billion dollars annually.

Working with the utility companies, Californians could retrofit all buildings in the state for maximum energy efficiency through:

• proper insulation
• solar panels to provide hot water heating
• R8 factor windows
• building modification and so on.

The further energy savings can release more funds for:

• planting more trees
• modernizing irrigation systems
• waste management
• sewage purification and the list goes on.

All of these activities will provide job opportunities for California workers transferring from pollution-connected jobs, and set an example for the rest of the nation and the whole world to follow.

REACTIVATING THE INITIATIVE IN ALL JURISDICTIONS

Keynote Address to the Midwest Academy, July 29, 1990

by Ira Arlook

I want to talk about doing initiatives everywhere we can, as soon as possible. This is hardly a new idea, even for those of us who don't live in California. We've gone back and forth over the past couple of years on this, but let's face it, in most cases, in most places, it's probably the best way out of governmental paralysis on so many of the issues we care about.

Several weeks ago, I read yet another account of how a state legislature is run on what the newspaper called a "pay-to-play" basis. A reporter happened to be in a hotel conference room packed with 200 nursing home operators. A veteran State Representative was making his fundraising pitch, to wit, and I quote:

"If you want the . . . Legislature to take care of your business needs, be sure to send money—and lots of it," to himself and other up-and-coming legislators whom he described as "a new generation of leaders for the '90s." He went on, "Now's the time to get your agenda in. If you don't think you can afford to give, consider all the ways state government can help or harm your bottom line. You can't afford not to. WE DON'T MAKE DECISIONS DOWN AT BROAD AND HIGH {STREETS} ON THE BASIS OF MERIT. MERIT IS INCIDENTAL. So reach into your pocket for a handful of money, reach deep . . . give early, give often. That's the fuel that feeds the machine."

From the reporter's point of view, the issue was that this bozo was an emissary of the Speaker of the House and the President Pro

Tem of the Senate, who run a cash-and-carry business that offers companies whatever they're willing to pay for. It looks like the Speaker controls the process.

Looked at from the perspective of business leaders, it's just another day at the office, another business expense. It's irritating to have those rascals upping the ante all the time, but thank God you can solve your political problems by throwing money at them.

For us, however, it's legislative gridlock. Almost invariably, no bill passes that affects a significant industry without that industry's prior agreement, and nothing worthwhile is ever agreed to. Of course, there are exceptions, but they prove the rule. In Louisiana, for example—by most measures, the nation's worst toxic swamp: first in toxic discharges into the water, 165 million pounds; first in toxic discharges into the ground via deep-well injection, an astounding 425 million pounds; and fourth in toxic air pollution, a mere 135 million pounds—an excellent law was passed last year over the objection of the chemical industry that aims at reducing toxic air emissions by 50% by 1995. Very good—but more than just a day late and a dollar short. The public wants and needs far, far more than this. Our Baton Rouge canvassers hear it at the door every night. People live in a perpetual state of high anxiety about their own and their children's health, surrounded as they are by many of the world's largest chemical plants. Things are moving far too slowly, when they move at all.

This is our greatest challenge—to overcome the governmental paralysis that prevents us from doing so many of the things that we, and our members, and most Americans, generally, want to do. The disparity between what the public wants and what legislators are willing to enact is enormous and growing, and nowhere is that truer than with the environment. [Health care, of course, is right up there, too.] We know this, but it's worth reviewing just one more recent poll. Media General and Associated Press found that four out of five respondents said pollution threatens the quality of their lives, and 75% said current anti-pollution laws are too weak. Most faulted state, local and federal environmental efforts. The level of concern was essentially unchanged from a poll that asked some of the same questions a year ago. Just two indicators of how strong people's feelings are:

- 70% favored election of a state environmental sheriff to go after polluters; and
- The same number supported banning pesticides that cause cancer in laboratory animals "even if the risk to humans is very slight."

California is a good example of both what is wrong and what to do about it. For the past decade the legislature has been nearly irrelevant. In recent years, it has been unable to enact measures even when they enjoyed virtually universal public support. Observers in California attribute most of the governmental paralysis to a legislature too beholden to powerful industries to regulate them in the public interest.

They compare it to the years at the turn of the last century when the Southern Pacific Railroad ran the California legislature. In 1910, Hiram Johnson campaigned for Governor with the slogan "Get the Southern Pacific out of politics!" In his inaugural address as Governor he called for the establishment of initiatives. And now in California for the past decade—particularly in the past four years—initiatives have been used, mostly with happy results, to do what the legislature would not do.

In 1986, a broad coalition of environmental and citizens' organizations, including in a leading role our affiliate Campaign California, passed Proposition 65. Although outspent $24 million to $1.8 million, it passed with 58% of the vote. It enacted strong provisions such as a prohibition against discharging any one of a long list of toxic and carcinogenic chemicals into the water, and a requirement that the public be warned in a written, visible way of any exposure to toxic or carcinogenic chemicals, anywhere.

Clearly one of the most far-reaching environmental laws ever passed at the state level. But it still did not exhaust the possibilities for reducing and cleaning up pollution. Which is why that same coalition is back with another, equally ambitious ballot measure called, as many of you know, BIG GREEN, which will eventually pass. It would, among other things:

- Phase out chemicals that destroy the ozone layer;
- Phase out the use of pesticides on food which have been proven to cause cancer or birth defects;

- Protect drinking water and coastal waters from toxic chemical contamination;
- Create an environmental advocate's office which can bring legal action to enforce all laws relating to environmental protection and public health.

This is why I'm spending so much time talking about what may appear to be merely a tactic. Compare what it has achieved and is likely to achieve in California since 1986 with what you think you are likely to get passed by your state legislature in the foreseeable future, and what you have helped pass already—combined.

Usually, at these events we're supposed to talk about vision and goals, and strategy. Tactics are assumed to follow, logically [and only get mentioned in workshops]. But if you look at our history as an organization, if you look at our most significant achievements—they came when we found effective tactics that we then generalized into a strategy. In a way, we found strategies that enabled us to make the best use of the successful tactic. Tactics dictated strategy.

Which now makes sense to me, although it never used to: when you start with a strategy, and then develop the tactics, you invariably wind up with many different tactics. Most of them turn out to be ineffective, not surprisingly, because they weren't chosen because they would work. They were chosen to support the strategy. When we start with tactics, we're often better grounded in reality, in what works.

For example, we started canvassing 15 or so years ago as a tactic to raise money. It worked. It worked not only to raise money, but to recruit members, to do grassroots lobbying, to affect elections, to make people feel connected, effective, hopeful.

We then incorporated the tactic into the fabric of our organizations, and we made it one of our key strategic ideas—to enable large numbers of diverse citizens to act on their own behalf, in an organized, focused, and effective way. We've been able to build a new institution in American civic life—the mass-membership citizens' organization, whose members are a microcosm of the American people. An institution that can draw people together and act across a broad range of economic and environmental issues on a durable and consistent basis.

If we hadn't found the tactic, we wouldn't have had a workable strategy for accomplishing all of this.

So back to the tactic. I know initiatives are double-edged swords. Some very bad things have been passed by initiative, and in California, for that matter. And once you have passed a good one, there are many ways in which a reluctant or hostile administration and bureaucracy can sabotage it. It is not a panacea. But on issues like pollution prevention where the public is so far ahead of where the political leadership is willing to go, where the need for action is so great, and where the state legislative route is blocked, we have little choice.

There are still two major problems. First, initiatives are not permitted in many states. Second, they cost a great deal of money. Let me deal with each of these in turn. First, where can we do initiatives, and what can we expect if we win in at least a majority of the places in which we try?

There are 21 states in which the kinds of initiatives we can use are permitted, excluding California. These states have a combined population of 73 million. There are 13 more states in which cities are permitted to do initiatives, which adds another 69 million people.

Passing significant pollution-prevention initiatives in any substantial fraction of these states and cities is, of course, worthwhile in its own right. But the likely effect that winning will have on our ability to negotiate seriously with major toxic polluters in other, non-initiative states will be substantial. Many of the major polluters operate in more than one state—some where we will pass initiatives, some where we won't. They can agree to major pollution reduction or square off against us at the ballot box and take their chances. State legislative bag men will not be able to mediate the relationship, and buffer and protect the polluters. Corporations will have to take us much more seriously than they ever have. We will win some important victories without, in all cases, having to go to the ballot. Power relationships will change.

And then there's money. It is important to stress that you can't go to the ballot unless you can raise enough money for a reasonable chance to win. Half-baked efforts do more harm than good. If you lose, the other side gets to claim that the public agrees with them. My estimate is that to run viable initiative campaigns in many of these states and big cities will require anywhere from a quarter of a million dollars in medium-sized cities to $1.5 million in states like Ohio and Michigan, and perhaps $2 million in Florida. This is daunting. Many of us in this room spend a great deal of our waking hours and devote a lot of our dreams to figuring out ways to raise enough money just to do what we do currently. This leads to the question of priorities, and therefore to strategy. Is what we are currently doing so worthwhile and so likely to be successful that it should take precedence over devoting ourselves to environmental initiatives where we can? Is hiring another organizer, working for yet another candidate, promoting a comprehensive state legislative agenda for the next session, or whatever, more likely to make a major contribution to shifting power relationships? This is not just another thing to do along with everything else we typically undertake. It's too large, and the stakes are too high.

What I'm advocating is that we change direction a bit. This is not unprecedented in our history. Ten years ago we had to decide to be involved in electoral politics. This change would come at a time when we have grown to appreciable size and strength. We have significant organizational resources to bring to initiative battles that are extremely important and that we have never had before:

1. We can put initiatives on the ballot in most states very inexpensively through our canvasses. And most of the people who sign the initiative petitions our canvassers carry become our members and are therefore kept in closer contact with developments in the campaign than under the normal circumstances in which signatures are gathered.

2. We have very large memberships that care about the issues we would put on the ballot and that are a large and growing portion of the likely voters in any election—and even more so in an initiative vote. We already include in our organizational budgets the substantial amounts of money necessary to send them excellent newsletters and updates.

3. We have built up considerable sophistication and expertise in running election campaigns—voter contact including door-to-door, mail, radio and TV—which will mean we do not have to spend large sums going outside our organizations to hire people to run the campaigns for us.

4. We have the ability to build and sustain the strong coalitions of diverse organizations necessary to wage successful initiative efforts. A major portion of our organizational success over the past decade has been based on coalition-building.

So, we don't have to wait on legislatures. We don't have to wait on the next Presidential election. We don't have to spread ourselves so thin with issue agendas that are too large.

But we do have to raise more money than we ever have in order to make it happen. If all that stands between us and a major breakthrough on the environment, in our ability to affect policy—our power as a democratic movement—is a few million dollars, we can't permit ourselves to fail.

We can wage and win breakthrough initiative battles in 1992. As events are shaping up, this will likely be the most interesting thing happening then. It's a challenge that we have to meet if we are to make our work of the past two decades bear fruit. It is not enough that Citizen Action is undergoing explosive growth that will take its membership from over 2 million members up to 5 million by the end of 1992. It is not enough that in just the last 6 months the number of state organizations and offices which are part of Citizen Action has jumped from 24 to 30, with another 6 or 7 likely over the next year-and-a-half. Wonderful, but not sufficient.

All this promise has to be realized in the form of major advances on our issues. And we can do this only if we change course. If it means spending the political capital we have accumulated over the years, what better way to spend it? If it means straining or breaking some of the political relationships we have nurtured carefully over the years, so be it. If it means risking our organizations, what have we built them for? Our heroes are the people who have taken risks, who have put all of themselves on the line in the service of their convictions.

It's a challenge we can meet, if we will only rise to it.

THE URUGUAY ROUND VERSUS SUSTAINABLE DEVELOPMENT

from *Recolonization: GATT, the Uruguay Round and the Third World*
by Chakravarthi Raghavan

Editors' Preface:
South-North Relations and the Uruguay Round

Many of the greatest environmental problems, from the destruction of tropical forests to the spread of deserts, are occuring in Third World nations. Global environmental problems can only be solved through the full cooperation of developing countries. For example, if present trends continue, fossil fuel burning in the Third World will become the major driving force for global warming by a few decades into the 21st century.

Development programs from the U.S. and other rich nations to aid the poor nations are in a state of disarray. The landscape is littered with ecologically disastrous impacts of the failures of official development efforts to reach the poor. Completely new approaches are needed.

A new intellectual framework for guiding future development efforts has already emerged in *Our Common Future*, the report of the World Commission on Environment and Development published in 1987. An estimated half-million copies of the report have been printed in twenty-five languages, and twenty-two countries have broadly accepted its concept of environmentally "sustainable development." This kind of development is much broader than the concept of development as "economic growth." It focuses on economic well-being brought about in ways that do not undermine ecological systems, which of course, once destroyed, limit economic growth for all the world's peoples. It also embraces goals of human development which may not necessarily flourish in traditional development policy: a long and healthy life, access to knowledge, political freedom, and human rights.

To make it possible for developing countries to pursue a strategy of sustainable development, we will have to face a painful fact of life. Present international economic arrangements, put in place mainly by the industrialized nations, are causing wealth to flow mostly from poor developing countries of the Third World to the developed world. The industrialized nations are still using the countries of the Third World as cheap labor and manufacturing markets, and as natural resources to be plundered. Northern hemisphere media provide almost no sense of the importance of the problem, but it is a major preoccupation in the Third World. The structure and rules of the entire international trading system will have to be revised to stop this "wealth drain" from the poor to the rich, and to help the Third World invest in environmentally sustainable development.

In the past few years, a major effort to rewrite the rules of international trade has been underway, called the Uruguay Round of trade negotionations under the auspices of the General Agreement on Tariffs and Trade (GATT). From a Third World point of view, these negotiations threaten to make the international rules of trade even more favorable to multinational corporations in the industrialized nations and more inimical to policies which would further self-reliance, non-dependence on foreign currency and exports, and the goals of sustainable development.

The selection below is from Chakravarthi Raghavan's *Recolonization: GATT, the Uruguay Round and the Third World* (Third World Network). Raghavan is an Indian journalist generally regarded as the leading interpretor of the GATT trade negotiations to Third World leaders and intellectuals. A past Editor-in-Chief of *The Press Trust* of India, he has been since 1980 Chief Editor of the daily *South-North Development Monitor* in Geneva. He argues that the policies of the Economic North are on a collision course with sustainable development in the Economic South.

Paul Rothkrug and Robert L. Olson

On September 20, 1986, at the South American seaside summer holiday resort town of Punta del Este (Uruguay), Ministers of Contracting Parties to the General Agreement on Tariffs and Trade (GATT) launched the Uruguay Round of Multilateral Trade Negotiations, the eighth under GATT auspices.

The wisdom of launching the new round and its contents had been the subject of acrimonious debate between the U.S. and other Industrialized Countries on the one side and the Third World countries on the other. It is no exaggeration to say that the Third World countries were virtually dragged into the negotiations, much against their will and better judgement.

The following year, at the United Nations General Assembly in New York, representatives of these same governments joined others (not members of GATT) in calling for "sustainable and environmentally sound development." This was in response to the Brundtland Commission report *Our Common Future*, the work of the World Commission on Environment and Development (WCED), chaired by Mrs. Gro Harlem Brundtland, Prime Minister of Norway. The Commission had published its report in March 1987 and had forwarded it to the General Assembly and all the UN bodies and specialized agencies.

This special independent Commission was set up in 1984 as a result of a UN General Assembly inititive to formulate a "global agenda for change."

While the Brundtland Commission did not challenge the fundamentals of the market economy, it did not endorse the received dogma, either. The 'Sustainable Development' advocated by the report, it has to be underlined, does not merely amount to safeguarding the environment from industrial pollution or saving the rain forests to prevent greenhouse effects or reducing or eliminating chlorofluorocarbons to arrest ozone depletion or even birth control to reduce population growth in the Third World. It is all these and very much more—a dimension that is often ignored.

In view of some of the narrow interpretations put on the report, the possibility of new conditionalities being imposed on the Third World countries became very evident. Hence, the General Assembly, while calling upon UN bodies to "take account" of the report and pursue 'sustainable development', repeatedly qualified all this with the phase "in accordance with their development plans, priorities and objectives."

After the publication of the report, Mrs. Brundtland carried the campaign of the report and its recommendations to various UN bodies — among others to the UN Conference on Trade and Development, the International Labour Conference, and the World Health Organization — and got their endorsement and support for 'sustainable development.'

The executive board of the World Bank, as well as the various regional banks and agencies, have all come out in support of 'sustainable development' and have said that 'environmental' considerations are being taken into account in their lending policies and programmes (making it however merely another 'conditionality' or an external decoration to their philosophies of market economy development based on deregulation and other dogmas).

The setting up of the Environmental Commission and the embracing of 'environmentalism' by the leading industrial countries of the North was a partial response to the growing concerns over ecological considerations among the peoples of the North and South. The ecology movements, particularly of the South, started as responses to local micro problems of water pollution, forest resource depletion and rights of indigenous peoples. But gradually they began to relate their problems at micro level to macro-policies of economic development and the market economy-led linear development models propagated by the international development agencies and international financial institutions like the World Bank.

The latter, particularly after the report of the WCED have also begun to speak of environmental considerations, but largely these have been external embellishments to the continued advocacy of resource-intensive (and inherently wasteful) linear development models and programmes based on the market. Deregulation and the withering away of government from the economic sectors plays a key role in these models. To some extent some of the Northern NGOs have allowed themselves to be co-opted by the Bank and their own national aid agencies and have agreed to deliver programmes on environment which have been used to mask the contents of the old development programmes with their heavy bias in favour of those who already enjoy economic superiority.

But both the ecology movements of the North and the South, which have related environmental degradation to the development policies and models of the World Bank and other development institutions, have not yet been able to relate their problems to the kind of trade policies and activities fostered by the GATT secretariat and its versions of 'free trade', that form the core of the Uruguay Round.

The GATT itself has not so far formally endorsed the concept of 'sustainable development', and it does not figure among the objectives of the new Round either. Mrs. Brundtland has not so far carried her fight into GATT, nor have the Nordic governments who have been trying to get other organizations to adopt the WCED Report.

Perhaps all this is no accident.

For the two philosophies, that behind the new round (and one which leading Industrial Nations and the officials of GATT advocate) and the philosophy of 'sustainable development' are not easily reconcilable. The basic premise behind the Uruguay Round, and the new GATT that would emerge out of it, is that left to themselves private enterprise and the transnational corporations function efficiently and for the benefit of all. Thus governments' powers to intervene and regulate need to be curbed.

Our Common Future accepts that the State, governments and the international community have to intervene to ensure sustainable development — to eradicate poverty, ensure justice for the poor who are outside the market, to regulate market forces, to make protection of the environment 'profitable' and penalize, and/or otherwise make unprofitable, the degradation of the environment.

REAGAN'S AMERICA: A CAPITAL OFFENSE

by Kevin P. Phillips

The 1980s were the triumph of upper America—an ostentatious celebration of wealth, the political ascendancy of the rich and a glorification of capitalism, free markets and finance. Not only did the concentration of wealth quietly intensify, but the sums involved took a megaleap. The definition of who's rich—and who's no longer rich—changed as radically during the Reagan era as it did during the great nouveaux riches eras of the late 19th century and the 1920s, periods whose excesses preceded the great reformist upheavals of the Progressive era and the New Deal.

But while money, greed and luxury became the stuff of popular culture, few people asked why such great wealth had concentrated at the top and whether this was the result of public policy. Political leaders, even those who professed to care about the armies of homeless sleeping on grates and other sad evidence of a polarized economy, had little to say about the Republican Party's historical role: to revitalize capitalism but also to tilt power, government largess, more wealth and income toward the richest portion of the population.

The public, however, understood and worried about this Republican bias, if we can trust late '80s opinion polls; nevertheless, the Democrats largely shunned the issue in the '88 election, a reluctance their predecessors also displayed during Republican booms of the Gilded Age of the late 19th century and the Roaring Twenties.

As the decade ended, too many stretch limousines in Manhattan, too many yacht jams off Newport Beach and too many fur coats in Aspen foreshadowed a significant shift of mood. Only for so long would strung-out $35,000-a-year families enjoy magazine articles about the hundred most successful businessmen in Dallas, or television shows about greed and glitz. Class structures may be weak in the United States, but populist sentiments run high. The political pendulum has swung in the past, and may be ready to swing again.

Indeed, money politics—be it avarice of financiers or the question of who will pay for the binges of the '80s—is shaping up as a prime theme for the 1990s. As we shall see, there is a historical cycle to such shifts: Whenever Republicans are in power long enough to transform economic policy from a middle-class orientation to capitalist overdrive, the Right gets so far ahead that a popular reaction inevitably follows, with the Democrats usually tagging along, rather than leading.

But this time, the nature of the reaction against excess is likely to be different. The previous gilded ages occurred when America was on the economic rise in the world. The 1980s, on the other hand, turned into an era of paper entrepreneurialism, reflecting a nation consuming, rearranging and borrowing more than it built. For the next generation of populists who would like to rearrange American wealth, the bad news is that a large amount of it has already been redistributed—to Japan, West Germany and to the other countries that took Reagan-era I.O.U.s and credit slips.

Society matrons, Wall Street arbitrageurs, Palm Beach real-estate agents and other money-conscious Americans picking up *USA Today* on May 22, 1987, must have been at first bewildered and then amused by the top story. In describing a Harris survey of the attitudes of upper-bracket citizens, the article summed up the typical respondent as "rich. Very. He's part of the thinnest economic upper crust: households with incomes of more than $100,000 a year."

A surprising number of 1980s polls and commentaries contributed to this naive perception—that "rich" somehow started at $50,000 or $100,000 a year, and that gradations above that were somehow less important. The truth is that the critical concentration of wealth in the United States was developing at higher levels—decamillionaires, centimillionaires, half-billionaires and billionaires. Garden-variety American millionaires had become so common that there were about 1.5 million of them by 1989.

In fact, even many families with what seemed like good incomes—$50,000 a year, say in Wichita, Kan., or $90,000 a year in New York City (almost enough to qualify as "rich," according to *USA Today*) —found it hard to make ends meet because of the combined burden of Federal Income and Social Security taxes, plus the soaring costs of state taxes, housing, health care and children's education. What few understood was that real economic status and leisure-class purchasing power had moved higher up the ladder, to groups whose emergence and relative affluence Middle America could scarcely comprehend.

No parallel upsurge of riches had been seen since the late 19th century, the era of the Vanderbilts, Morgans and Rockefellers. It was the truly wealthy, more than anyone else, who flourished under Reagan. Calculations in a Brookings Institution study found that the share of national income going to the wealthiest 1 percent rose from 8.1 percent in 1981 to 14.7 percent in 1986. Between 1981 and 1989, the net worth of the Forbes 400 richest Americans nearly tripled. At the same time, the division between them and the rest of the country became a yawning gap. In 1980, corporate chief executive officers, for example, made roughly 40 times the income of average factory workers. By 1989, C.E.O.s were making *93 times as much.*

Finance alone built few billion-dollar fortunes in the 1980s relative to service industries like real estate and communications, but it is hard to overstate Wall Street's role during the decade, partly because Federal monetary and fiscal policies favored financial assets and because deregulation promoted new debt techniques and corporate restructuring.

Selling stock to retail clients, investment management firms or mutual funds paid well; repackaging, remortgaging or dismantling a Fortune 500 company paid magnificently. In 1981, analysts estimate, the financial community's dozen biggest earners made $5 million to $20 million a year. In 1988, despite the stock-market collapse the October before, the dozen top earners made $50 million to $200 million.

The redistribution of American wealth raised questions not just about polarization, but also about trivialization. Less and less wealth was going to people who produced something. Services were ascendant—from fast food to legal advice, investment vehicles to data bases. It is one thing for new technologies to reduce demand for obsolescent professions, enabling society to concentrate more resources in emerging sectors like health and leisure. But the distortion lies in the disproportionate rewards to society's economic, legal and cultural manipulators—from lawyers and financial advisers to advertising executives, merchandisers, media magnates and entertainers.

A related boom and distortion occurred in nonfinancial assets— art and homes, in particular. Art and antiques appreciated fourfold in the Reagan era, to the principal benefit of the richest 200,000 or 300,000 families. Similar if lesser explosions in art prices took place in the Gilded Age and in the 1920s. While the top one-half of 1 percent of Americans rolled in money, the luxuries they craved—from Picassos and 18th-century English furniture to Malibu beach houses— soared in markets virtually auxiliary to those in finance.

Meanwhile, everyone knew there was pain in society's lower ranks, from laid-off steelworkers to foreclosed farmers. A disproportionate number of female, black, Hispanic and young Americans lost ground in the 1980s, despite the progress of upscale minorities in each category. According to one study, for example, the inflation-adjusted income for families with children headed by an adult under 30 collapsed by roughly one-fourth between 1973 and 1986.

Even on an overall basis, median family and household incomes showed only small inflation-adjusted gains between 1980 and 1988. Middle America was quietly hurting too.

While corporate presidents and chairmen feasted in the 1980s, as many as 1.5 million midlevel management jobs are estimated to have been lost during those years. Blue-collar America paid a larger price, but suburbia, where fathers rushed to catch the 8:10 train to the city, was counting its casualties, too. "Middle managers have become insecure," observed Peter F. Drucker in September 1988, "and they feel unbelievably hurt. They feel like slaves on an auction block."

American transitions of the magnitude of the capitalist blowout of the 1980s have usually coincided with a whole new range of national economic attitudes. Evolving government policies—from tax cuts to high interest rates—seem distinct, but they are actually linked. Whether in the late 19th century, the 1920s or the 1980s, the country has witnessed conservative politics, a reduced role for government, entrepreneurialism and admiration of business, corporate restructuring and mergers, tax reduction, declining inflation, pain in states that rely on commodities like oil and wheat, rising inequality and concentration of wealth, and a buildup of debt and speculation. The scope of these trends has been impressive—and so has their repetition, though the two periods of the 20th century have involved increasingly more paper manipulation and less of the raw vigor typical of the late 19th-century railroad and factory expansion.

Federal policy from 1981 to 1988 enormously affected investment, speculation and the creation and distribution of wealth and income, just as in the past.

The reduction or elimination of Federal income taxes was a goal in previous capitalist heydays. But it was a personal preoccupation for Ronald Reagan, whose antipathy toward income taxes dated back to his high-earning Hollywood days, when a top tax bracket of 91 percent in the '40s made it foolish to work beyond a certain point. Under him, the top personal tax bracket would drop from 70 percent to 28 percent in only seven years. For the first time since the era of Franklin D. Roosevelt, tax policy was fundamentally rearranging its class loyalties.

Reaganite theorists reminded the country that the Harding-Coolidge income-tax cuts—from a top rate of 73 percent in 1920 to 25 percent in 1925—helped create the boom of the '20s. Back then, just as in the '80s the prime beneficiaries were the top 5 percent of Americans, people who rode the cutting edge of the new technology of autos, radios and the like, emerging service industries, including new practices like advertising and consumer finance, a booming stock market and unprecedented real-estate development. Disposable income soared for the rich, and with it, conspicuous consumption and financial speculation. After the 1929 crash and the advent of the New Deal, tax rates rose again; the top rate reached 79 percent by 1936 and 91 percent right after the war. In 1964, the rate fell in two stages, to 77 percent and then to 70 percent.

Under Reagan, Federal budget policy, like tax changes, became a factor in the realignment of wealth, especially after the 1981-'82 recession sent the deficit soaring. The slack was made up by money borrowed at home and abroad at high cost. The first effect lay in who received more government funds. Republican constituencies—military producers and installations, agribusiness, bondholders and the elderly—clearly benefited, while decreases in social programs hurt Democratic interests and constituencies: the poor, big cities, housing, education. Equally to the point, the huge payments of high-interest charges on the growing national debt enriched the wealthy, who bought the bonds that kept Government afloat.

Prosperous individuals and financial institutions were beneficiaries of government policies in other ways. Starting in the Carter years, Congress began to deregulate the financial industry; but the leap came in the early 1980s, when deposit and loan interest ceilings were removed. To attract deposits, financial institutions raised their interest rates, which rose and even exceeded record postwar levels. The small saver profited, but the much larger gain, predictably, went to the wealthy. (The benefits of high interest were intensified, of course, by the declining maximum tax rate on dividend and interest income. The explosion of after-tax unearned income for the top 1 percent of Americans was just that—an explosion.)

The savings and loan crisis now weighing on American taxpayers also had roots in deregulation. Before 1982, savings and loan associations were required to place almost all their loans in home mortgages, a relatively safe and stable class of assets. But in 1982, after soaring interest rates turned millions of low-interest mortgages into undesirable assets, a new law allowed savings and loans to invest their funds more freely—100 percent in commercial real-estate ventures if they so desired. Like banks in the 1920s, many thrifts proceeded to gamble with their deposits, and by 1988, many had lost. Gamblers and speculators enriched themselves even as they stuck other Americans with the tab.

Reagan's permissiveness toward mergers, antitrust enforcement and new forms of speculative finance was likewise typical of Republican go-go conservatism. Unnerving parallels were made between the Wall Street raiders of the 1980s—Ivan Boesky and T. Boone Pickens—and the takeover pools of the 1920s, when high-powered operators would combine to "boom" a particular stock. For a small group of Americans at the top, the pickings were enormous.

An egregious misperception of late 20th-century politics is to associate only Democrats with extremes of public debt. Before 1933, conservatives—Federalists, Whigs and Republicans alike—sponsored government indebtedness and used high-interest payments to redistribute wealth upward.

In addition, Republican eras were noted for a huge expansion of private debt. In the 1920s, individual, consumer and corporate debt kept setting record levels, aided by new techniques like installment purchases and margin debt for purchasing securities. In the kindred '80s, total private and public debt grew from $4.2 trillion to more than $10 trillion. And just as they had 60 years earlier, new varieties of debt became an art form.

Government fiscal strategists were equally loose. In part to avoid the deficit-reduction mandates of the Gramm-Rudman-Hollings Act, they allowed Federal credit programs, including student and housing loans, to balloon from $300 billion in 1984 to $500 billion in 1989.

In contrast to previous capitalist blowouts, the fast-and-loose federal debt strategies of the '80s did not simply rearrange assets within the country but served to transfer large amounts of the nation's wealth overseas as well. America's share of global wealth expanded in the Gilded Age and again in the 1920s. The late 1980s, however, marked a significant downward movement: one calculation, by the Japanese newspaper *Nihon Deizai Shimbun*, had Japan overtaking the United States, with estimated comparative assets of $43.7 trillion in 1987 for Japan, versus $36.2 trillion for the United States.

The United States was losing relative purchasing power on a grand scale. There might be more wealthy Americans than ever before, but foreigners commanded greater resources. On the 1989 Forbes list of the world's billionaires, the top 12, with the exception of one American, were all foreigners—from Japan, Europe, Canada and South Korea. Dollar millionaires, once the envy of the world, were becoming an outdated elite.

This shift partly reflected the ebb of America's postwar preeminence. Yet the same Reagan policies that moved riches internally also accelerated the shift of world wealth, beginning with the budget deficits of the early 1980s but intensifying after the ensuing devaluation of the dollar from 1985 to 1988.

If the devalued dollar made the Japanese, French and Germans relatively richer, it also increased their purchasing power in the United States, turning the country into a bargain basement for overseas buyers. This is the explanation for the surging foreign acquisition of properties, from Fortune 500 companies to Rockefeller Center in Manhattan and a large share of the office buildings in downtown Los Angeles.

The dollar's decline also pushed per capita gross national product and comparative wages in the United States below those of a number of Western European nations. The economist Lester C. Thurow summed up the predicament: "When it comes to wealth, we can argue about domestic purchasing power. But, in terms of international purchasing power, the United States is now only the ninth wealthiest country in the world in terms of per capita G.N.P. We have been surpassed by Austria, Switzerland, the Netherlands, West Germany, Denmark, Sweden, Norway and Japan."

Not everyone looked askance at foreign wealth and investment. American cities and states welcomed it. From the textile towns of South Carolina to the rolling hills of Ohio, foreigners were helping declining regions to reverse their fate. Yet as Warren Buffett, the investor, said: "We are much like a wealthy family that annually sells acreage so that it can sustain a life style unwarranted by its current output. Until the plantation is gone, it's all pleasure and no pain. In the end, however, the family will have traded the life of an owner for the life of a tenant farmer."

Nowhere was Japanese investment more obvious than in Hawaii, where real-estate moguls from Tokyo pronounced the property they were grabbing up "almost free." An economist at a Hawaiian bank warned that the state was "a kind of test lab for what's facing the whole country." Indeed, in 1988, broader foreign ambitions were apparent. The author Daniel Burstein quoted Masaaki Kurokawa, then head of Japan's Nomura Securities International, who raised with American dinner guests the possibility of turning California into a joint U.S.-Japanese economic community.

Public concern over America's international weakness had been a factor in Ronald Reagan's election back in 1980. Voters had wanted a more aggressive leader than Jimmy Carter. For various reasons, the great things promised were not delivered. Reagan could re-create a sense of military prowess with his attacks on Grenada and Libya. But in the global economy he took a country that had been the world's biggest creditor in 1980 and turned it into the world's largest debtor. Despite opinion polls documenting public concern about this erosion, surprisingly little was made of the issue in the 1988 Presidential campaign, possibly because the Democrats could not develop a coherent domestic and international alternative.

Much of the new emphasis in the 1980s on tax reduction and the aggressive accumulation of wealth reflected the Republican Party's long record of support for unabashed capitalism. It was no fluke that three important Republican supremacies coincided with and helped generate the Gilded Age, the Roaring Twenties and Reagan-Bush years.

Part of the reason survival-of-the-fittest periods are so relentless, however, rests on the performance of the Democrats as history's second-most enthusiastic capitalist party. They do not interfere with capitalist momentum, but wait for excesses and the inevitable popular reaction.

In the United States, elections arguably play a more important cultural and economic role than in other lands. Because we lack a hereditary aristocracy or Establishment, our leadership elites and the alignment of wealth are more the product of political cycles than they are elsewhere. Capitalism is maneuvered more easily in the United States, pushed in new regional and sectoral directions. As a result, the genius of American politics—failing only in the civil War—has been to manage through ballot boxes the problems that less-fluid societies resolve with barricades and with party structures geared to class warfare.

Because we are a mobile society, Americans tolerate one of the largest disparities in the industrial world between top and bottom incomes, as people from the middle move to the top, and vice versa. Opportunity has counted more than equality.

But if circulating elites are a reality, electoral politics is an important traffic controller. From the time of Thomas Jefferson, the nation has undulated in 28- to 36-year waves as each watershed election puts a new dominant region, culture, ideology or economic interest (or combination) into the White House, changing the country's direction. But after a decade or two, the new forces lose touch with the public, excessively empower their own elites and become a target for a new round of populist reform. Only the United States among major nations reveals such recurrent electoral behavior over two centuries.

But it is the second stage—dynamic capitalism, market economics and the concentration of wealth—that the Republican Party is all about. When Republicans are in power long enough, they ultimately find themselves embracing limited government, less regulation of business, reduced taxation, disinflation and high real interest rates. During America's first two centuries, these policies shaped the three periods that would incubate the biggest growth of American millionaires (or, by the 1980s, billionaires). History suggests that it takes a decade or more for the Republican party to shift from broad middle-class nationalism into capitalist overdrive, and the lapse of 12 years between the first Nixon inauguration of 1969 and the first Reagan inauguration repeats this transformation.

Nixon, like the previous Republican nationalist Presidents Abraham Lincoln and William McKinley, was altogether middle class, as was his "new majority" Republicanism. He had no interest in unbridled capitalism during this 1969-74 Presidency.

In fact, many of the new adherents recruited for the Republican coalition in 1968 and 1972 were wooed with the party's populist attacks on inflation, big government, social engineering and the Liberal Establishment. Many Republican voters of that era embraced outsider and anti-elite values, and like similar participants in previous Republican national coalitions, they would become uneasy in the 1980s as Reagan or Bush Republicanism embraced Beverly Hills or Yale culture and the economics of leveraged buyouts, not of Main Street.

Besides this uneasiness, reflected in opinion polls, a second sign that a conservative cycle is moving toward its climax has been the extent to which Democratic politics has been cooperative: when wealth is in fashion, Democrats go along. The solitary Democratic president of the Gilded Age, Grover Cleveland, was a conservative with close Wall Street connections. In the '20s, the Democratic presidential nominees in both 1920 (James Cox, an Ohio publisher) and

1924 (John W. Davis, a corporate lawyer) were in the Cleveland mold. Alfred E. Smith, who ran in 1928, would eventually oppose Roosevelt and the New Deal. In the '20s Congressional Democrats competed with Republicans to cut upper-bracket and corporate taxes.

Fifty years later, Jimmy Carter, the only Democratic President to interrupt the long Republican hegemony since 1968, was accused by the historian Arthur M. Schlesinger, Jr., of an "eccentric effort to carry the Democratic Party back to Grover Cleveland." Despite his support for substantial new Federal regulation, Carter clearly deviated from his party's larger post-New Deal norm. He built foundations that would become conservative architecture under Reagan: economic deregulation; capital-gains tax reduction and the right-money policies of the Federal Reserve. (The Fed's chairman, Paul A. Volcker, was a Carter appointee.) Congressional Democrats even echoed their policies of the 1920s by colluding in the bipartisan tax-bracket changes of 1981 and 1986.

Thus, the Democrats could hardly criticize Reagan's tax reductions. For the most part, they laid little groundwork for an election-year critique in 1988, leaving the issue to Jesse Jackson, whose appeal was limited by his race and third-world rhetoric, and to noncandidates like Mario M. Cuomo. Michael S. Dukakis was obviously uncomfortable with populist politics. Though several consultants and economists urged him to pick up the theme of economic inequality, Dukakis made competence, not ideology, his initial campaign issue. Only in late October, with his campaign crumbling, did the Democratic candidate reluctantly convert to a more traditional party line. It came too late.

Republican strategists could hardly believe their luck. Said Lee Atwater, Bush's campaign manager, after the election: "The way to win a Presidential race against the Republicans is to develop the class-warfare issue, as Dukakis did at the end—to divide up the haves and have-nots and to try to reinvigorate the New Deal coalition and to attack."

On the surface, this was a missed Democratic opportunity. But the lesson of history is that the party of Cleveland, Carter and Dukakis has rarely rushed its anti-elite corrective role. There would be no rush again in 1988—nor, indeed, in 1989.

Early in his Presidency, George Bush replaced the Coolidge portrait hung by Ronald Reagan in the White House with one of Theodore Roosevelt, reflecting Bush's belief in T.R.'s commitment to conservation, patrician reform and somewhat greater regulatory involvement.

Yet there has not been too much evidence of a kinder, gentler America beyond softer, more conciliatory rhetoric. The budget remained unkind to any major expansion of domestic programs, and Bush's main tax objective was a reduction in the capital-gains rate, a shift that critics said would continue to concentrate benefits among the top 1 percent of Americans.

By spring 1990, Washington politicians confronted the most serious debt- and credit-related problems since the bank failures, collapsed stock prices, farm foreclosures and European war debt defaults of the Great Depression. From the savings and loan associations bailout to junk bonds, from soaring bankruptcies and shaky real-estate markets, to Japanese influence in the bond market, Federal policy makers were forced to realize that a crucial task—and peril—of the 1990s would involve cleaning up after the previous decade's credit-card parties and speculative distortions.

In May, the facade of successful deficit reduction crumbled as Administration officials confessed that bailing out insolvent savings and loans could cost as much as a half-trillion dollars. It became clear that taxes would have to rise. In California, where the anti-tax revolt began more than a decade ago, the approval by the state's votes earlier this month [June, 1990] of an increase in the gasoline tax was seen by many as a sign of public willingness to come to grips with the fiscal deficiencies of the 1980s.

Even some Democrats who previously collaborated with Republican economics have begun to argue that the rich who had made so much money in the '80s should bear a larger share of the new burdens of the '90s. A number of Republicans share this disquiet. The Senate minority leader, Bob Dole of Russell, Kan., insisted in late 1989 that if the White House wanted to cut capital-gains taxes for the prosperous, it should also raise the minimum wage for the poor. Last month, the House Republican leader, Robert H. Michel of Peoria, Ill., was reported to favor an increase in the tax rate for the top

1 percent of Americans, from 28 percent to 33 percent. The second-ranking Republican leader in the House, Newt Gingrich of Georgia, suggested in April that conservatives, too, had to develop some ideas for economic redistribution.

Meanwhile, opinion poll after opinion poll has shown lopsided voter support for raising the income-tax rate for people making more than $80,000, $100,000 or $200,000. The 1990s seem ready to reflect a new anti-Wall Street, anticorporate and antigreed outlook set forth in books (and coming movies) like "Bonfire of the Vanities," "Liar's Poker" and "Barbarians at the Gate."

Nor was the changing mood apparent only in the United States. Kindred psychologies and political analysis could also be seen in other countries like Britain, Japan and Canada, where 1980s financial and real-estate booms likewise concentrated wealth in the hands of the very rich and increased economic inequity. A headline last month in the *Financial Times* of London could have been written in the United States: "The Rich Get Nervous."

Whether the populist reactions that followed past boom periods recur in the '90s no one can know. But there could be no doubt that the last decade ended as it had begun: with a rising imperative for a new political and economic philosophy, and growing odds that the 1990s will be a very different chapter than the 1980s in the annals of American wealth and power.

(Originally published in *The New York Times Magazine*, June 17, 1990)

REALITIES 1990

Facts excerpted from the Pulitzer Prize-nominated *Diet for a New America* by John Robbins

The diet of North Americans has changed significantly since 1900. At that time most meals were based on grains, potatoes, fresh vegetables and fruit—meat was consumed only occasionally and in small amounts. This dietary style was rich in fiber and complex carbohydrates and low in refined sugars. In recent years we have replaced this diet with one based upon high-fat, low-fiber foods—namely meat, dairy and other animal products.

By 1985, Americans were eating half the amount of grains and potatoes they ate in 1909, while their beef consumption had increased by almost half, and their poultry consumption increased by over 280 percent.[1] Such drastic dietary changes cannot occur without significant consequences—not only in our health, but in the economy and the environment as well.

Here are some realities about the health and ecological effects of our meat-centered diet:

Amount of corn grown in United States consumed by human beings:
20%[2]

Amount of corn grown in United States consumed by livestock:
80%[2]

Amount of soybeans grown in United States consumed by livestock:
90%[2]

How frequently a child on Earth dies as a result of malnutrition:
Every 2.3 seconds[3]

•

Pounds of grain and soybeans needed to produce
1 pound of edible food from:
Beef 16[4]
Pork 6[4]
Turkey 4[4]
Chicken/Egg 3[4]
Number of children who die as a result of malnutrition every day:
38,000[3]

•

Amount of nutrient wasted by cycling grain through livestock:
Protein 90%[5]
Carbohydrate 99%[5]
Fiber 100%[5]
Number of people who will die as a result of malnutrition this year:
20,000,000[6]

•

Pounds of edible product that can be produced
on an acre of prime land:
Cherries 5,000[7]
Green beans 10,000[7]
Apples 20,000[7]
Carrots 30,000[7]
Potatoes 40,000[7]
Tomatoes 50,000[7]
Celery 60,000[7]
Beef 250[7]
Number of complete vegetarians who can be fed on the amount of
land needed to feed 1 person consuming a meat-based diet: **15**[5]

•

Amount of U.S. cropland producing livestock feed: **64%**[8]

Amount of U.S. cropland producing fruits and vegetables: **2%**[8]

Number of people who could be adequately nourished using the
land, water and energy that would be freed from growing livestock
feed if Americans reduced their intake of meat by 10%:
100,000,000[9]

•

Historic cause of demise of many great civilizations:
Topsoil depletion[10]

Amount of original U.S. topsoil lost to date: **Over two-thirds**[11]

Current annual topsoil loss on agricultural land in the U.S.: **Over 5 billion tons**[12]

Amount of U.S. topsoil lost from cropland, pasture, rangeland and forest land directly associated with livestock raising : **85%**[13]

•

Number of acres of U.S. forest which have been cleared to create cropland, pastureland and rangeland currently producing a meat-centered diet: **260,000,000**[14]

Number of acres of U.S. land which could be returned to forest if Americans adopted a meat-free diet and ceased exporting livestock feed: **204,000,000**[14]

Number of acres of U.S. land which could be returned to forest for each American who adopts a meat-free diet: **0.8**[14]

•

Calories of fossil fuel expended to produce 1 calorie of protein from beef: **78**[15]

Calories of fossil fuel expended to produce 1 calorie of protein from soybeans: **2**[15]

•

User of more than half of all water consumed for all purposes in the United States:
Livestock production[16]

In California, the number of gallons of water needed to produce 1 edible pound of:
Tomatoes 23[7]
Lettuce 23[7]
Potatoes 24[7]
Wheat 25[7]
Carrots 33[7]
Apples 49[7]
Oranges 65[7]
Grapes 70[7]
Milk 130[7]

Egg 544[7]
Chicken 815[7]
Pork 1630[7]
Beef 5214[7]

How long it takes a person to use 5200 gallons of water showering
(at 5 showers per week, 5 minutes per shower, with a flow rate
of 4 gallons per minute): **One year**

•

Amount of all raw materials (base products of farming, forestry,
and mining; including fossil fuels) consumed by the U.S. that are
devoted to the production of livestock: **One-third**[17]

•

A driving force behind the destruction of the tropical rainforests:
American meat habit[18]

Amount of meat imported annually by U.S. from Central and
South America: **300,000,000 pounds**[19]

Percentage of Central American children under the age of five
who are undernourished: **75**[20]

Current rate of species extinction due to destruction of tropical
rainforests and related habitats: **1,000/year**[21]

•

Production of excrement by U.S. livestock: **230,000 lbs/second**[22]

Water pollution attributable to U.S. agriculture including runoff of
soil, pesticides and manure: **Greater than all municipal and
industrial sources combined**[23]

•

Number of U.S. medical schools: **125**[24]

Number of U.S. medical schools with a required course in
nutrition: **30**[24]

Training in nutrition received during 4 years of medical school by
average U.S. physician: **2.5 hours**[25]

Most common cause of death in U.S.: **Heart disease**[26]

How frequently a heart attack strikes in U.S.: **Every 25 seconds**[27]

How frequently a heart attack kills in U.S.: **Every 45 seconds**[27]

Risk of death from heart attack for average American man: **50%**[27]

Risk of death from heart attack for American man
who consumes no meat: **15%**[28]

Risk of death from heart attack for American man who consumes
no meat, dairy products or eggs: **4%**[28]

Amount you reduce your risk of heart attack by reducing your
consumption of meat, dairy products and eggs by 10%: **9%**[28]

Amount you reduce your risk of heart attack by reducing your
consumption of meat, dairy products and eggs by 50%: **45%**[28]

Amount you reduce your risk of heart attack by reducing your
consumption of meat, dairy products and eggs by 100%: **90%**[28]

Rise in blood cholesterol from consuming 1 egg per day: **12%**[29]

Rise in heart attack risk from 12% rise in blood cholesterol: **24%** [29]

Average cholesterol level of people eating a meat-centered diet:
210 mg/dl[30]

Chance of dying from heart disease if you are male and your blood
cholesterol is 210 mg/dl: **Greater than 50%**[31]

Leading sources of saturated fat and cholesterol in American diets:
Meat, dairy products and eggs[32]

Cholesterol found in all grains, legumes, fruits,
vegetables, nuts, seeds: **None**

Chance of dying from heart disease if you do not consume
cholesterol: **4%**[28]

World populations with high meat intakes who do not have
correspondingly high rates of colon cancer: **None**[33]

World populations with low meat intakes who do not have
correspondingly low rates of colon cancer: **None**[33]

Increased risk of breast cancer for women who eat eggs daily
compared to once a week: **2.8 times higher**[34]

Increased risk of breast cancer for women who eat meat daily
compared to less than once a week: **3.8 times higher**[34]

Increased risk of fatal ovarian cancer for women who eat eggs 3 or
more days a week compared to less than once a week:
3 times higher[35]

Milk Producer's original ad campaign slogan:
"Everybody needs milk"[36]

What the Federal Trade Commission called the "Everybody needs milk" slogan: **"False, misleading and deceptive"**[36]

Milk Producer's revised campaign slogan: **"Milk has something for everybody"**[36]

Increased risk of breast cancer for women who eat butter and cheese 2-4 times a week compared to once a week: **3.2 times higher**[34]

Increased risk of fatal prostate cancer for men who consume meats, dairy products and eggs daily as compared to sparingly: **3.6 times higher**[37]

•

Recommended amount of daily calories to be derived from protein according to World Health Organization: **4.5%**[38]

Recommended amount of daily calories to be derived from protein according to Food and Nutrition Board of the U.S.D.A.: **6%**[39]

Recommended amount of daily calories to be derived from protein according to National Research Council: **8%**[40]

Amount of calories as protein in Human milk: **5%**[41]

Amount of calories as protein in rice: **8%**[42]

Amount of calories as protein in wheat: **17%**[42]

Amount of calories as protein in broccoli: **45%**[42]

Disease linked to inadequate protein consumption: **Kwashiorkor**[43]

Number of cases of kwashiorkor in United States: **Virtually none**[43]

Diseases linked to excess animal protein consumption: **Osteoporosis**[44] **and kidney failure**[45]

Number of cases of osteoporosis and kidney failure in the United States: **Tens of millions**[44, 45]

The average measurable bone loss of female meat-eaters at age 65: **35%**[44]

The average measurable bone loss of female vegetarians at age 65: **18%**[44]

Person who popularized the concept that vegetarians need to combine proteins: **Frances Moore Lappé**[46]

Frances Moore Lappé's updated research on a healthy, varied vegetarian diet: **Protein combining is unnecessary**[46]

Health status of pure vegetarians from many populations of the
world according to the Food and Nutrition Board of the
National Academy of Sciences: **Excellent**[47]

•

Meat Board advertisements claim: **Today's meats are low in fat.**
Their ad campaigns show servings with: **200 calories**
Reality:
**The servings of beef they show us are half the size of an average
serving and have been surgically defatted with a scalpel**[48]

•

The dairy industry claims: **Whole milk is 3.5% fat**
Reality:
**That 3.5% figure is based on weight and most of the weight in
milk is water; the amount of calories provided by fat in
whole milk is 50%**[49]

•

Dairy industry advertising claim:
Milk is nature's most perfect food
Reality:
**Milk is nature's most perfect food for a calf,
who has four stomachs, will double its weight in 47 days,
and can weigh up to 1000 pounds within a year**[50]

•

Dairy industry advertising claim:
To grow up big and strong, drink lots of milk
Reality:
**The enzyme necessary for digestion of milk is lactase. 20% of
Caucasians and up to 90% of Black and Asian people have no
lactase in their intestines, causing cramps, bloating and
diarrhea upon drinking milk**[51]

•

The meat, dairy and egg industries tell us:
Animal products constitute 2 of the 4 "Basic food groups"
Reality:
**There were originally 12 official "Basic food groups"
before these industries applied enormous political pressure
on behalf of their products**[52]

The meat, dairy and egg industries tell us:
We are well-fed only with animal products.

Reality:
The diseases which can be commonly prevented, consistently
improved, and sometimes cured by a low-fat diet,
free from animal products, include[53]

Strokes	Heart disease	Osteoporosis
Prostate cancer	Breast cancer	Colon cancer
Hypertension	Trichinosis	Salmonellosis
Hypoglycemia	Peptic ulcers	Endometrial cancer
Diabetes	Hemorrhoids	Obesity
Asthma	Constipation	Diverticulosis
Irritable colon syndrome		Gallstones

•

Amount of U.S. mothers' milk containing
significant levels of DDT: **99%**[54]

Amount of U.S. vegetarian mothers' milk containing
significant levels of DDT: **8%**[54]

Average chemical pollution of breast milk in U.S. women
compared to complete vegetarians according to one study
published in the New England Journal of Medicine:
35 times higher[55]

Percentage of male college students sterile in 1950: **0.5**[56]

Percentage of male college students sterile in 1978: **Up to 25**[56]

Sperm count of average American male compared to 30 years ago:
Down 30%[56]

Major contributor to sterility and sperm count reduction
in U.S. males: **Chlorinated hydrocarbon pesticides,
including dioxin, DDT, etc.**[57]

Meat industry advertising claims the dioxin and other pesticides in
today's beef are not a concern because: **The quantities are so small**

Reality:
A mere ounce of dioxin could kill 1 million people[58]

Common belief:
**U.S. Department of Agriculture protects our health
through meat inspection**

Reality:
Less than 1 out of every quarter million slaughtered animals is tested for toxic chemical residues[59]

•

The dye used for many years by the U.S. Department of Agriculture to stamp meats "Choice", "Prime", or "U.S. No. 1":
Violet Dye No. 1

Current status of Violet Dye No. 1
Banned as proven carcinogen[60]

•

Amount of total antibiotics used in U.S. fed routinely to livestock:
55%[61]

•

Staphylococci infections resistant to penicillin in 1960: **13%[61]**
Staphylococci infections resistant to penicillin in 1988: **91%[61]**
Major contributing cause:
Breeding of antibiotic-resistant bacteria in factory farms due to routine feeding of antibiotics to livestock[61]

•

Effectiveness of antibiotics:
Declining rapidly[61]
Major contributing cause:
Breeding of antibiotic-resistant bacteria in factory farms due to routine feeding of antibiotics to livestock[61]

•

Response by entire European Economic Community to routine feeding of antibiotics to livestock: **Ban[61]**
Response by American meat and pharmaceutical industries to routine feeding of antibiotics to livestock:
Full and complete support[61]

•

Only man to win Ironman Triathalon more than twice:
Dave Scott, 6-time winner
Food choices of Dave Scott: **Vegetarian**

•

World record holder for 24-hour triathalon, swim 4.8 miles,
cycle 185 miles, run 52.5 miles: **Sixto Linares**
Food choices of Sixto Linares: **Complete vegetarian**

•

Other notable vegetarian athletes:

- **Paavo Nurmi:** 20 World records in distance running,
9 Olympic medals
- **Robert Sweetgall:** World's premier ultra-distance walker
- **Murray Rose:** World records—400 and 1500 meter freestyle
- **James and Jonathan de Donato:** World records—distance
butterfly stroke swimming
- **Bill Pickering:** World record—swimming the English Channel
- **Estelle Gray and Cheryl Marek:** World record—cross-country
tandem cycling
- **Henry Aaron:** All-time major league baseball home run
champion
- **Robert Parish:** Starting center for Boston Celtics, at age 36,
7'0", 260 lbs.
- **James Donaldson:** Starting center for Dallas Mavericks, 7'3"
290 lbs.
- **Stan Price:** World record—bench press
- **Andreas Cahling:** Winner—Mr. International body building
championship
- **Roy Hilligan:** Winner—Mr. America body building
championship
- **Ridgely Abele:** Winner—8 national championships in Karate,
including U.S. Karate Association World Championship

Sources:

1 Committee on Diet and Health, Food and Nutrition Board,
Commission of Life Sciences, National Research Council; Diet and
Health, Implications for Reducing Chronic Disease Risk; National
Academy Press, Washington, D.C., 1989, pg. 57   2 United States
Department of Agriculture; Agricultural Statistics 1989; United States
Government Printing Office, Washington, D.C., 1989, pg. 31, Table
40—Corn: Supply and Disappearance, United States 1974–88; pg. 125,

Table 168—Soybeans: Supply and Disappearance, United States, 1974–88 • Ahalt, J. Dawson, Chairman, World Food and Agricultural Outlook and Situation Board, U.S. Department of Agriculture, July 1980 as cited in Lappé, Frances Moore, *Diet for a Small Planet*, tenth anniversary edition, Ballantine Books, New York, 1982, pg. 92 • Soyfoods Industry and Market: Directory and Databook; Soyfoods Center, 1985   3 UNICEF "State of the World's Children"   4 U.S. Department of Agriculture, Economic Research Service, Beltsville, Maryland as cited by Lappé, as per note 2, pg. 70 • Altschul, Aaron, *Proteins: Their Chemistry and Politics*, Basic Books, 1965, pg. 264 • Dovring, Folke, "Soybeans," *Scientific American*, Feb. 1974   5 Lappé, as per note 2, pg. 69 • "The World Food Problem," A Report by the President's Science Advisory Committee, vol. II, May, 1967 • FACT SHEET, Food Animals Concern Trust, Issue No. 26, Nov. 1982, Chicago • Resenberger, Boyce, "Curb on U.S. Waste Urged to Help the World's Hungry," *NY Times*, Oct. 25, 1974 • "World Food Crisis: Basic Ways of Life Face Upheaval from Chronic Shortages," *NY Times*, Nov. 4, 1974, pg. 14   6 Institute for Food and Development Policy • Oxfam America   7 Aldridge, Tom, and Schlubach, Herb; *Soil and Water*, Fall 1978, No. 38, Water Requirements for Food Production, University of California Cooperative Extension, pgs. 13–17 • Erlich, Paul and Anne, *Population, Resources, Environment*, W.H. Freeman, 1972, pgs. 75–76   8 U.S. Department of Agriculture; Agricultural Statistics 1989; pg. 390, Table 554—Crops: Area, Yield, Production and Value, United States, 1986–88, pg. 31   9 Lester Brown of the Worldwatch Institute cited by Resenberger, as per note 5, adjusted using 1988 figures from United States Department of Agriculture, Agricultural Statistics 1989, Table 74—High Protein Feeds, and Table 75—Feed Concentrates Fed to Livestock and Poultry   10 Carter, Vernon Gill, and Dale, Tom, *Topsoil and Civilization*, Rev. ed., Norman, Univ. of Oklahoma Press, 1974   11 Brune, William, State Conservationist, Soil Conservation Service, Des Moines, Iowa, testimony before Senate Committee on Agriculture and Forestry, July 6, 1976 • King, Seth, "Iowa Rain and Wind Deplete Farmlands," *NY Times*, Dec. 5, 1976, pg. 61 • Harnack, Curtis, "In Plymouth County, Iowa, The Rich Topsoil's Going Fast, Alas," *NY Times*, July 11, 1980 • Hur, Robin, "Six Inches from Starvation; How and Why America's Topsoil is Disappearing," *Vegetarian Times*, March, 1985, pgs. 45–47   12 United States Department of Agriculture, Soil Conservation Service, Iowa State University Statistical Laboratory, Statistical Bulletin Number 790, Summary Report 1987, National Resources Inventory, December 1989 • United States

Department of Agriculture, Miscellaneous Publication Number 1482; The Second RCA Appraisal, Soil, Water and Related Resources on Non-Federal Land in the United States: Analysis of Condition and Trends, June 1989 **13** Hur, Robin, quoted by Lappé, as per note 2, pg. 80 **14** Hur, Robin, and Fields, David, "Are High-Fat Diets Killing our Forests?", *Vegetarian Times*, Feb. 1984 **15** David and Marcia Pimentel, Food, Energy and Society, 1979, pg. 59 • David Pimentel et al., "Energy and Land Constraints in Food Protein Production," *Science*, Nov. 21, 1975 **16** Soil Degradation: Effects on Agricultural Productivity, Interim Report Number Four of the National Agricultural Lands Study, 1980, and Fact Book of U.S. Agriculture, U.S. Dept. of Agriculture, Misc. Publication No. 1065, Nov. 1979, Table 3, cited by Lappé, as per note 2, pg. 76 **17** Raw Materials in the United States Economy, Technical Paper 47, Vivian Spencer, U.S. Department of Commerce, U.S. Dept. of Interior, Bureau of Mines, 1977, pg. 3 **18** Parsons, James, "Forest to Pasture: Development or Destruction?" *Revista de Biologia Tropical*, Vol. 24, Supplement 1, 1976 • Myers, Norman, "Cheap Meat vs. Priceless Rainforests," *Vegetarian Times*, May, 1982 • De Walt, Billie, "The Cattle are Eating the Forest," Bulletin of the Atomic Scientists • The World Conservation Strategy: "The World Conservation Strategy in Brief," World Wildlife Fund, 1980 **19** U.S. Department of Commerce; "U.S. General Imports for Consumption" Schedule A, Commodity by Country of Origin, Customs and C.I.F. Values. Dec. 1987 **20** Robbins, John, *Diet for a New America*, pg. 353 **21** Rainforest Action Network, 301 Broadway, Suite A, San Francisco, CA • Ehrlich, Anne, Center for Conservation Biology, Dept. of Biological Sciences, Stanford University • *Acres, U.S.A.*, Kansas City, Missouri, Volume 15, No. 6, June, 1985, pg. 2 **22** Pimentel, David, "Energy and Land Constraints in Food Protein Production," *Science*, Nov. 21, 1975 • Jasiorowski, H.A., "Intensive Systems of Animal Production," Proceedings of the III World Conference on Animal Production, ed. R.L. Reid, Sydney, Sydney University Press, 1975, pg. 384 • Robbins, Jackie, Environmental Impact Resulting From Unconfined Animal Production, Environmental Protection Technology Series, Cincinnati, U.S.E.P.A., Office of Research and Development, Environmental Research Information Center, Feb. 1978, pg. 9 • *Environmental Science and Technology*, Vol. 5, No. 12, 1970, pg. 1098, cited by Lappé, as per note 2, pg. 69 **23** Cross, Russell H. and Byers, Floyd M., et al., "Current Issues in Food Production: A Perspective on Beef as a Component in Diets for Americans"; supported by the National Cattleman's Association, April 1990, pg. 5.26. **24** Kapleau, Phillip, *To Cherish All Life*, Harper and Row, SF, 1981, pg. 59

25 McDougall, John, *The McDougall Plan*, New Century Publishers, 1983, pg. 7   26 Walford, Roy, *Maximum Life Span*, W.W. Norton and Co., New York, London 1983, pg. 8   27 Gordon, T., "Premature Mortality from Coronary Heart Disease: The Framingham Study," *Journal of the American Medical Assoc.*, 215:1617, 1971 • Bainton, C., "Deaths From Coronary Heart Disease. . . ." *New England Journal of Medicine*, 268:569, 1963 • Kannel, W., "Incidence and Prognosis of Unrecognized Myocardial Infarction—An Update on the Framingham Study," *New England Journal of Medicine*, 311:1144, 1984   28 Hardinge, M., "Nutritional Studies of Vegetarians: IV. Dietary Fatty Acids and Serum Cholesterol Levels," *American Journal of Clinical Nutrition*, 10:522, 1962 • Phillips, R., "Coronary Heart Disease Mortality Among Seventh Day Adventists with Differing Dietary Habits," Abstract Amer. Public Health Assoc. Meeting, Chicago, Nov. 16–20, 1975 • Ruys, J., "Serum Cholesterol . . . in Australian Adolescent Vegetarians," *British Medical Journal*, 6027:87, 1976 • Sacks, F., "Plasma Lipids and Lipoproteins in Vegetarians and Controls," *New England Journal of Medicine*, 292:1148, 1975 • Sacks, F., "Blood . . . in Vegetarians," *American Journal of Epidemiology*, 100:390, 1974 • Armstrong, B., "Blood . . . ," *American Journal of Epidemiology*, 105:444, 1978 • Sirtori, C., "Soybean Protein Diet . . . ," *Lancet*, 8006:275, 1977 • Barrow, J., "Studies in Atherosclerosis . . . ," *Annals of Internal Medicine*, 52:372, 1960 • Phillips, R., "Coronary Heart Disease . . . Differing Dietary Habits: A Preliminary Report," *American Journal of Clinical Nutrition*, 31:181, 1978 • Walles, C., "Hold the Eggs and Butter: Cholesterol is Proved Deadly and Our Diet May Never be the Same," *Time*, March 26, 1984, pg. 62   29 Sacks, F., "Ingestion of Egg Raises Plasma Low Density Lipoproteins in Free-Living Subjects," *Lancet*, 1:647, 1984   30 McDougall, J., as per note 25, pg. 56   31 *ibid.*   32 Hausman, P., *Jack Sprat's Legacy—The Science and Politics of Fat and Cholesterol*, Richard Marek Publishers, NY, 1981   33 Wynder, E., "Dietary Fat and Colon Cancer," *Journal of the National Cancer Institute*, 54:7, 1975 • Berg, J., "Can Nutrition Explain the Pattern of International . . . Cancers"? *Cancer Research*, 35:3345, 1975 • Wynder, E., "The Dietary Environment and Cancer," *Journal of the American Dietitians Assoc.*, 71:385, 1977 • Weisburger, J., "Nutrition and Cancer—On the Mechanisms Bearing on Causes of Cancer of the Colon, Breast, Prostate, and Stomach," *Bulletin of the NY Academy of Medicine*, 56; 673, 1980 • Mann, G., "Food Intake and Resistance to Disease," *Lancet*, 1:1238, 1980 • Reddy, B., and Wynder, E., "Large Bowel Carcinogenisis: Fecal Constituents of Populations with Diverse Incidence

of Colon Cancer," *Journal of the National Cancer Institute*, 50:1437, 1973 • Hill, M., "Bacteria and the Aetiology of Cancer of the Large Bowel," *Lancet*, 1:95, 1971 • Reddy, B., "Nutrition and Its Relationship to Cancer," *Advances in Cancer Research*, 32:237, 1980 • Reddy, B., "Metabolic Epidemiology of Large Bowel Cancer," *Cancer*, 42:2832, 1978 • Hill, M., "Colon Cancer: A Disease of Fiber Depletion or of Dietary Excess," *Digestion*, 11:289, 1974 • Walker, A., "Colon Cancer and Diet with Special References to Intakes of Fat and Fiber," *Amer. Journal of Clinical Nutrition*, 34:2054, 1981 • Cummings, J., "Progress Report: Dietary Fiber," *Gut*, 14:69, 1983 • Phillips, R., "Role of Lifestyle and Dietary Habits in Risk of Cancer . . . ," *Cancer Research*, 35:3513, 1975 • Hardinge, M., "Nutritional Studies of Vegetarians: III. Dietary Levels of Fiber," *American Journal of Clinical Nutrition*, 6:523, 1958 • Weisburger, J., "Colon Cancer—Its Epidemiology . . . ," *Cancer*, 40:2414, 1977 • Haenszel, W., "Studies of Japanese Migrants, I. Mortality from Cancer . . . ," *Journal of the National Cancer Institute*, 40:43, 1968 • *Journal of the National Cancer Institute*, Dec. 1973, pg. 1771   **34** Hirayama, Takeshi, Paper presented at the Conference on Breast Cancer and Diet. U.S.-Japan Cooperative Cancer Research Program, Fred Hutchinson Center, Seattle, WA., Mar. 14–15, 1977   **35** Snowden, John, *Journal of the American Medical Association*, July 19, 1985   **36** Oski, F., *Don't Drink Your Milk*, Wyden Books, 1977, pg. 6   **37** Hill, P., "Environmental Factors of Breast and Prostatic Cancer," *Cancer Research*, 41:3817, 1981   **38** "Protein Requirements," Food and Agriculture Organization, World Health Organization Expert Group, United Nations Conference, Rome, 1965 • Pfeiffer, C., *Mental and Elemental Nutrients*, Keats, 1975   **39** Food and Nutrition Board, Recommended Daily Allowances, Washington, D.C., National Academy of Sciences.   **40** National Research Council, *Recommended Dietary Allowances*, 9th ed., Washington, D.C., National Academy of Sciences, 1980, pg. 46   **41** *Textbook of Physiology and Biochemistry*, 4th ed., Williams and Wilkens, Ballantine, 1954, pgs. 167–170. Adapted in McDougall, J., *The McDougall Plan*, New Century Publishers, 1983, pg. 101   **42** "Nutritive Value of American Foods in Common Units," U.S. Department of Agriculture Handbook No. 456.   **43** Hardinge, M., et al., "Nutritional Studies of Vegetarians: Part V, Proteins . . . ," *Journal of the American Dietetic Association*, Vol. 48, No 1, Jan. 1966, pg. 27 • Hardinge, M., et al., "Nutritional Studies of Vegetarians: Part I, . . ." *Journal of Clinical Nutrition*, Vol. 2, No. 2, March/April, 1984, pg. 81 • Hausman, P., "Protein: Enough is Enough," *Nutrition Action*, Oct. 1977, pg. 4 • Food and Nutrition Board, "Vegetarian Diets,"

Washington, DC: National Academy of Sciences, 1974, pg. 2 • Hegsted, D., cited in Register, U.D., et al., "The Vegetarian Diet," *Journal of the American Dietetic Association*, 62(3):255, 1973 • Nicol, B., et al., "The Utilization of Proteins and Amino Acids in Diets Based on Cassava . . . ," *British Journal of Nutrition*, 111:1430, 1981 • McLaren, D., "The Great Protein Fiasco," *Lancet*, 2:93, 1974 • Gopalan, C., "Effect of Calorie Supplementation on Growth of Undernourished Children," *American Journal of Clinical Nutrition*, 26:563, 1973 • McLaren, D., "A Fresh Look at Protein-Calorie Malnutrition," *Lancet*, 2:485, 1966   44 Allen, L., "Protein-induced hypercalcuria: a longer term study," *American Journal of Clinical Nutrition*, 32:741, 1979 • Brockis, J., "The effects of vegetable and animal protein diets on calcium, urate, and oxalate excretion," *Br J Urology*, 54:590, 1982. • Barzel, V., *Osteoporosis*, Grune and Stratton, New York, 1970   45 Brenner, B., "Dietary protein intake and the progressive nature of kidney disease: The role of hemodynamically mediated glomerular injury in the pathogenesis of progressive glomerular sclerosis in aging, renal ablation and intrinsic renal disease," *New England Journal of Medicine*, 307:652, 1982 • Maschio, G., "Effects of dietary protein and phosphorus restriction on the progression of early renal failure," *Kidney Int*, 22:371, 1982   46 Lappé, Francis Moore, as per note 2, pgs. 17, 162   47 Food and Nutrition Board, "Vegetarian Diets," Washington, D.C.: National Academy of Sciences, 1974, pg. 2   48 Liebman, B., The Center for Science in the Public Interest, in *Nutrition Action*, cited in *Vegetarian Times*, July, 1985   49 Hausman, P., as per note 32, pgs. 44–45   50 *Textbook of Physiology and Biochemistry*, 4th ed., Williams and Wilkens, Ballantine, 1954, pgs. 167–170. Adapted in McDougall, J., as per note 25, pg. 101 • Ensminger, M.E., *Beef Cattle Science*, 5th ed., Interstate Printers and Publishers, Danville, Ill., pg. 1034 • Roy Hull, University of California, Davis, Dept. of Animal Science   51 Gilat, T., "Lactase deficiency: the world pattern today," *Israel J Med Sci*, 15:369, 1979 52 Hausman, Patricia, as per note 32, pgs. 16–17, 25–39   53 For complete documentation, refer to: Robbins, John, *Diet for a New America*, Stillpoint, 1987 • McDougall, John, *McDougall's Medicine*, New Century Publishers, 1985 • McDougall, J., *The McDougall Plan*, New Century Publishers, 1983 54 "A Brief Review of Selected Environmental Contamination Incidents with a Potential for Health Effects," prepared by the Library of Congress for the Committee on Environment and Public Works, U.S. Senate, Aug. 1980, pgs. 173–174   55 *New England Journal of Medicine*, March 26, 1981   56 Richards, B., "Drop in Sperm Count is Attributed to Toxic Environment," *Washington Post*, Sept. 12, 1979 • Brody, J.,

"Sperm Found Especially Vulnerable to Environment," *NY Times*, March 10, 1981 • "Unplugging the Gene Pool," *Outside*, Sept. 1980 • Jansson, E., "The Impact of Hazardous Substances Upon Fertility Among Men in the U.S., and Birth Defects," *Friends of the Earth*, Washington, D.C., Nov. 17, 1980. **57** Dougherty, Ralph, Florida State University as cited in *Diet for a New America*, pg. 330 **58** Nordland, R., and Friedman, J., "Poison at our Doorstep," *Philadelphia Inquirer*, Sept. 23–28, 1979 **59** *Mainstream*, Summer 1983, pg. 17, USDA Statistical Summary: Federal Meat and Poultry Inspection for 1976, Jan. 1977 pg. 3 **60** United Press, "Food and Drug Administration: Meat Dye May Cause Cancer," *Washington Post*, April 6, 1973 **61** Molotsky, Irvin, "Animal Antibiotics Tied to Illnesses in Humans," *NY Times*, Feb. 22, 1987 • New Jersey State Health Department, Div. of Environmental Health, cited in Scharffenberg, J., *Problems with Meat*, Woodbridge Press, 1982, pg. 60 • Stoller, K., "Feeding an Epidemic," *Animals' Agenda*, May 1987, pgs. 32–33 • Schell, O., *Modern Meat*, Vintage Books, 1985

ABOUT THE AUTHORS

Paul Rothkrug has been in the life and health insurance business since 1947. He founded T.R. Paul, Inc., a firm specializing in life insurance, employee benefits, executive compensation, and pensions. T.R. Paul, Inc. operates throughout southern New England and eastern New York State and currently employees 106 people in Newton, Connecticut. Mr. Rothkrug retired in April, 1980 and moved to San Francisco. He started the Environmental Rescue Fund in 1988, a self-funded program working toward a comprehensive program of social, political and economic changes required to restore the environment as a habitat for life on Earth. *Mending the Earth* is the first completed project for the Fund.

Robert L. Olson is a Senior Associate at the Institute for Alternative Futures in Alexandria, Virginia. He works with local communities, associations, and corporate leaders on developing strategic visions of future success. A political scientist by training, he taught for several years at the University of Illinois and was a Resident Fellow at the University's Center for Advanced Study. He has worked previously with the Congressional Office of Technology Assessment and the National Research Council. In the early 1980s he chaired the Governing Council of the New World Alliance, the first attempt in the U.S. to create a national "green" political organization.

Nancy Skinner has been a Berkeley City Council member since 1984. Environmental activism provided her with her start in city politics. Dedicated to using the powers of local government to establish sound environmental policies, she recently coauthored "Model Ordinances for Environmental Protection." For the Fall 1990 U.N.-sponsored World Congress of Local Governments For A Sustainable

Future, she served on the charter committee which convened the conference, gave a workshop on waste reduction, and prepared case studies of the most innovative city-initiated environmental programs from across the globe. She is the Executive Director of Local Solutions to Global Pollution, an information and technical assistance clearinghouse in Berkeley, California.

Dr. Robert Costanza is an Associate Professor at the University of Maryland's Chesapeake Biological Laboratory, which is part of the Center for Environmental and Estuarine Studies (CEES). He is the chief editor of the new journal *Ecological Economics*. He is also president and co-founder (with Herman Daly) of the International Society for Ecological Economics. He has degrees in architecture and urban and regional planning, environmental engineering and systems ecology (with a minor in economics) from the University of Florida at Gainesville.

Lisa Wainger is a graduate research assistant at the Center for Environmental and Estuarine Studies (CEES), pursuing a doctoral degree in marine, estuarine, and environmental sciences. She has an undergraduate degree in earth sciences from the University of California at Santa Cruz and has worked as a science writer for the Smithsonian Institute and the American Geophysical Union.

Denis Hayes is Chairman and CEO of Green Seal, a non-profit organization that seeks to mobilize American consumers on behalf of environmental values. During the Carter Administration he was Executive Director of the Solar Energy Research Institute—then a 1,000-person federal laboratory with an annual budget of $130 million. He has authored more than 100 publications in the environmental field. His book, *Rays of Hope: The Transition to a Post-Petroleum World,* has been translated into six languages. He was awarded the 1979 Thomas Jefferson Medal, the highest award in the nation for public service by an individual under the age of 35.

Bill Keepin is an environment and energy consultant in Berkeley, California. His research focuses on strategies for abating global environmental problems, and his analyses have influenced energy policy debates in several countries. He holds M.S. and Ph.D. degrees in mathematical physics and applied mathematics and has held research positions at the International Institute for Applied Systems Analysis, Princeton University, Beijer Institute of the Royal Swedish Academy of Sciences, and Rocky Mountain Institute. Dr. Keepin has advised senior management of major oil companies and testified before the U.S. House of Representatives and the Australian government.

Ted Flanigan has been the Energy Program Director at Rocky Mountain Institute for the past four years, where he developed the COMPETITEK retainer service on advanced techniques for electric efficiency. COMPETITEK provides information on energy-efficient technologies and implementation to over 170 organizations in more than 40 countries around the world. He is presently Director of IRT, an energy and environmental consulting firm.

Anna Edey, a native of Sweden, is the designer and director of Solviva Solargreen Design on Martha's Vineyard, Massachusetts. She lectures and consults in the U.S. and Europe with support from the government of Denmark. A Solviva Winter Garden Greenhouse is now being created at Bornholm's Naturskole Grynebaekken on the island of Bornholm in the Baltic Sea in southern Denmark. She is currently at work on her first book, *How Shall We Live: Solutions For A World In Peril.*

John Todd was trained in agriculture, parasitology, and tropical medicine and received his doctorate in fisheries and oceanography. In 1969 he cofounded the New Alchemy Institute to create a science and practice based upon ecological precepts. In 1980 he founded Ocean Arks International, and in the same year received, with Nancy Jack Todd, the Swiss Threshold Award for their "contributions to human knowledge." In 1984 he began developing technologies for treating wastes and purifying water. In 1987 he was recognized by the United Nations Environmental Program for his "contributions toward protecting the Earth's environment." In 1989 he received The Chico Mendes Memorial Award from the United

States Environmental Protection Agency for his pioneering work in Solar Aquatics.

Nancy Jack Todd is Vice President of Ocean Arks International and Publisher and Editor of its newspaper, *Annals of Earth,* a publication dedicated to the dissemination of the ideas and practice of ecological sustainability throughout the world. She is currently at work on a book entitled *Daughters of Earth,* a scholarly and passionate tale of earth stewardship from the woman's perspective. Among her published works is *Bioshelters, Ocean Arks, City Farming: Ecology as the Basis for Design,* 1984, published by Sierra Club Books. In 1980 she shared the Swiss Threshold Award for "her contributions to human knowledge" with physicist David Bohn and John Todd, and in 1987 she was recognized by the United Nations Environmental Program for "her contributions in protecting the earth's environment."

Richard Register is President of Urban Ecology, which helps cities with creek restoration, street redesign, downtown planning, and ecological architecture. He is the author of *Ecocity Berkeley* (North Atlantic Books) and convened the First International Ecocity Conference in Berkeley in March, 1990.

Kathryn McCamant and **Charles Durrett** are community designers and authors of the book *Cohousing: A Contemporary Approach to Housing Ourselves* (Ten Speed Press, 1988) which introduced this European housing model to the United States. They are principals of The CoHousing Company, a San Francisco Bay Area design and consulting firm that works with resident groups and developers to build cohousing communities. Their work has received national recognition including interviews on ABC's "World News Tonight," NBC's "Today Show," and National Public Radio as well as articles in *The New York Times, Utne Reader, Architecture, The Christian Science Monitor* and the *Los Angeles Times.*

Ira Arlook is Executive Director and one of the founders of Citizen Action, a national federation of citizens' organizations in thirty-one states. Citizen Action provides practical opportunities for its members to get involved in their community on the toughest issues affecting them, from toxic waste to health and utility costs.

Kathy Glass is a Berkeley, California-based freelance writer and editor and environmental activist. She works with various organizations, including Earth Island Institute, Ancient Forest International, and the Japan Environmental Exchange. Her travel and environmental writing has appeared in such publications as *Oceanus, Sierra, Earth Island Journal, Earthwatch, Whole Earth Review*, and *The New York Times*. She is senior editor at North Atlantic Books in Berkeley, California.

Index

Advanced technology
  business opportunities of, 73
  elements of, 69, 72
  fundamental importance, 67
  green versus gray, 2
  misconceptions about, 64, 67
  nature as model, 67, 68, 69
  solar, 74-78
Automobile
  efficiency, 148
  liability insurance
    alternative based on worker's
      compensation, 162
    low yield to claimant, 161-162
    payment at the gas pump, 163-
      164
    possible savings, 163, 165
    use of savings, 167-168
  mass transit instead of, 166-167
  reduced role for, 149
  transitional vehicles, 165-166

Business opportunities
  from change, 16
  from new technology, 73
  from the ecological city, 127
  tax incentives toward, 17, 18

Change
  dysfunctional aspects, 7
  economic choice as instrument for,
    33-34, 49
  mobilizing for, 20-22
  need for local initiative, 23-25
  resistance to, 3
  ten year program for, 14-19
CoHousing
  democracy, 135, 136
  meeting diverse needs, 133-135

  the living community, 132, 137
Compelling necessity, 6
Cooking fuel, solar, 78
Cost versus value, 4

Debt
  as capital transfer tool, 187, 189-190
  U.S. as debtor nation, 189
  use of to avoid deficit reduction,
    187
Deserts
  arrest of, 153
  disappearance of, 16
Diet and nutrition, 194-203

Earth stewards, xvi, 4
Eastern Europe, xiii
Ecological decision making, 57, 58
Ecological engineering
  new professions from, 155
  through living machines, 109-120
Ecological literacy, xvii, xviii
Ecologically healthy cities, 126,127
  built for people, not cars, 125
  need for fundamental change, 124
  planning for, 126
  to reduce need for automobiles, 124
  to reduce transportation needs, 125
Efficiency
  bonus, 6
  competitiveness, 6, 86
  financing of, 92
  for automobiles, 148
  from living machines, 119-120
  from regulatory reform, 91
  implementation of, 90, 91
  previous experience, 85
  profit from, 84-85
  technology of, 86-90